What are Oxford Literature Companions?

Oxford Literature Companions is a series designed to provide you with comprehensive support for popular set texts. You can use the Companion alongside your play, using relevant sections during your studies or using the book as a whole for revision.

Each Companion includes detailed guidance and practical activities on:

- ● **Plot and Structure**
- ● **Context**
- ● **Genre**
- ● **Characterization and Roles**
- ● **Language**
- ● **Themes**
- ● **Performance**
- ● **Critical Views**
- ● **Skills and Practice**

How does this book help with exam preparation?

As well as providing guidance on key areas of the play, throughout this book you will also find 'Upgrade' features. These are tips to help with your exam preparation and performance.

In addition, in the extensive **Skills and Practice** chapter, the 'Exam skills' section provides detailed guidance on areas such as how to prepare for the exam, understanding the question, planning your response and hints for what to do (or not do) in the exam.

In the **Skills and Practice** chapter there is also a bank of **Sample questions** and **Sample answers**. The **Sample answers** are marked and include annotations and a summative comment.

How does this book help with terminology?

Throughout the book, key terms are highlighted in the text and explained on the same page. There is also a detailed **Glossary** at the end of the book that explains, in the context of the play, all the relevant literary terms highlighted in this book.

KT-468-842

Which edition of the play has this book used?

Quotations and character names have been taken from the Oxford School Shakespeare edition of *Othello* (ISBN 978-0-198-32873-5).

How does this book work?

Each book in the Oxford Literature Companions series follows the same approach and includes the following features:

- **Key quotations** from the play
- **Key terms** explained on the page and linked to a complete glossary at the end of the book
- **Activity boxes** to help improve your understanding of the text
- **Upgrade** tips to help prepare you for your assessment

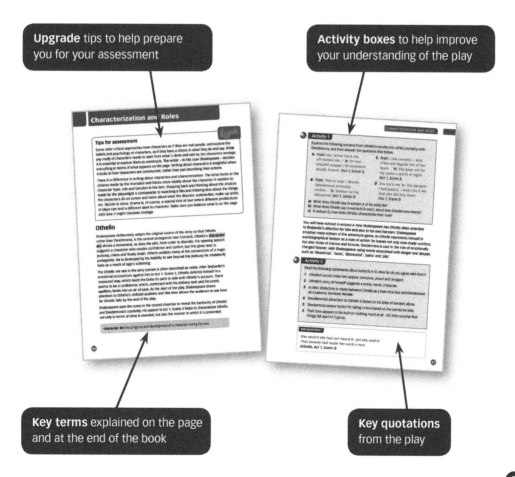

Upgrade tips to help prepare you for your assessment

Activity boxes to help improve your understanding of the play

Key terms explained on the page and at the end of the book

Key quotations from the play

Plot and Structure

Plot

Act 1, Scene 1

The opening scene, set on a street in Venice at night time, introduces the play's **antagonist**, Iago. He is in mid-conversation with Roderigo. The **dialogue** establishes important information about Iago's manipulative qualities and names other characters we meet later in the play. In lines 1–74, we learn that:

- Roderigo has paid Iago to secure a marriage between himself and Desdemona, a Venetian aristocrat.
- Roderigo is unhappy with Iago's efforts because Desdemona has married Othello the Moor. Brabantio, Desdemona's father, is unaware of the marriage.
- Othello, a general, has promoted Michael Cassio to be his lieutenant. Iago, Othello's 'ancient' or ensign, feels bitter about this and wants revenge. In reference to Othello, he openly admits, '**I follow him to serve my turn upon him**'.

In the next part of the scene, we see Iago at work. He encourages Roderigo to wake Brabantio and inform him that his daughter Desdemona has married. At first, Brabantio dismisses Roderigo – he has already insisted that Roderigo is not good enough for his daughter – but then he accepts that Roderigo is telling the truth.

Iago exploits the fact that Othello is a Moor, taking delight in tormenting Brabantio that his daughter is having sex with a '**black ram**'. The scene ends with Brabantio organizing people to apprehend his daughter and Othello.

The opening scene introduces several conflicts, the central feature of drama and narrative. This scene is rich in excitement – the action occurs at night time, intrigue is afoot, and rivalry and desire are apparent. On stage, characters appear carrying tapers (candles), Brabantio appears at a high window in his nightgown and, by the end of 184 lines, we have the prospect of confrontation.

antagonist a character, often a villain, who stands in opposition to the main character

dialogue the words spoken between characters

Key quotation

**Your heart is burst; you have lost half your soul;
Even now, now, very now, an old black ram
Is tupping your white ewe.**
(Iago)

Activity 1

We discover in the next scene that there is a wider political conflict between Venice and Turkey over Cyprus, but the opening scene is all about personal conflict. Make notes about the various conflicts. Consider:

- the nature of the conflict

- the relative status of the characters in conflict. Who has greater power?

- whose side – if any – the audience is invited to take.

Act 1, Scene 2

The setting switches to another part of town, outside Othello's lodgings. The audience knows that Brabantio is on his way to confront Othello. Notice how Iago, who exits before the end of Act 1, Scene 1, is present at the beginning of this scene, manipulating Othello and then Cassio.

- Iago tells Othello that there may be objections to his marriage.
- Cassio enters with a message to request Othello's urgent attendance at a meeting with the Duke about military problems in Cyprus.
- Othello briefly exits the stage, then Iago tells Cassio about the marriage.
- Othello re-enters, followed by Brabantio, Roderigo and Officers. Brabantio angrily accuses Othello of using witchcraft to ensnare Desdemona.
- Brabantio threatens Othello and wants him to be arrested, but realizes that the meeting with the Duke must take place first.

Activity 2

Look closely at Othello's responses to Brabantio's complaint.

a) Consider the following extracts and what they reveal about Othello's character.

> Let him do his spite;
> My services which I have done the signiory
> Shall out-tongue his complaints.
> *(Othello)*

> Keep up your bright swords, for the dew will rust them.
> Good signior, you shall more command with years
> Than with your weapons.
> *(Othello)*

> Hold your hands,
> Both you of my inclining and the rest.
> Were it my cue to fight, I should have known it
> Without a prompter. Where will you that I go
> To answer this your charge?
> *(Othello)*

b) Compare your responses to Othello with Iago's description of him in Act 1, Scene 1.

You could use a table like the one below to record your notes.

Extract	What it reveals about Othello's character	How it compares with Iago's description of Othello
1		

Act 1, Scene 3

The setting changes, this time to the Venetian council chamber. Issues of conflict are central once more, with the Duke carefully weighing up the differing reports about the Turkish fleet. He appears to be calm and able to make rational judgements, in contrast to Othello's later rashness.

- The Duke instructs Othello to lead the Venetian forces defending Cyprus.
- Brabantio repeats his accusations about Othello's manipulation of Desdemona.
- Othello defends himself and the Duke calls for Desdemona, who corroborates Othello's version of events. Brabantio agrees to withdraw his accusation.
- Arrangements are made for departure to Cyprus, with Desdemona travelling later with Iago and Emilia (Iago's wife and Desdemona's maid).
- Iago convinces a pessimistic Roderigo to go to Cyprus for the opportunity of securing Desdemona. Iago reveals in a **soliloquy** that there is an unproven rumour that Othello had sex with Emilia.

Othello's account of his courtship is dignified and eloquent. Structurally, it is separated into two sections: 'Most potent, grave, and reverend signiors… I won his daughter' and 'Her father lov'd me… let her witness it'. By the end the Duke acknowledges that Othello's tale would 'win my daughter too'.

The entrance of Desdemona is a key event in the play. Up to this point, her attitudes and behaviour have been related by the various men in her life. Her respectful but forthright acknowledgement that she has a 'divided duty' to her father and her husband, yet must choose Othello, seems fair. Brabantio's loss of power is obvious here. Othello's ability to give space to his wife to speak contrasts **ironically** with his later refusal to listen to her.

Desdemona (Irène Jacob) and Othello (Laurence Fishburne) defend their marriage in front of Brabantio and the Duke in the 1995 film *Othello*

ironically from irony, implying a secondary meaning, often revealing the truth of a situation

soliloquy a speech delivered by a character alone on stage

Key quotation

Look to her, Moor, if thou hast eyes to see:
She has deceiv'd her father, and may thee
(Brabantio)

Activity 3

Consider the account of Othello and Desdemona's relationship that they offer in this scene. Some critics have suggested that it is unusual. Explore:

- the nature of their attraction towards each other
- the process of their courtship and their differences in race and status
- the way Desdemona's character seems at odds with her father's view of her.

Act 2, Scene 1

The action of the play now moves to Cyprus.

- A storm at sea destroys the Turkish fleet. The ships carrying the Venetians land at different times, with Cassio's ship arriving first.
- Cassio praises Othello and Desdemona to Montano, governor of Cyprus. Iago, Desdemona and Emilia then arrive. Iago, seemingly light-heartedly, complains about the wanton, deceitful ways of women.
- Cassio acts courteously towards Desdemona and appears to touch her hand, something Iago plans to use for manipulative purposes.
- Othello arrives, greeting Desdemona fondly, which contrasts with the bitter **asides** from Iago, which focus on his desire to destroy their joy.
- Iago persuades Roderigo that Desdemona is in love with Cassio. Roderigo agrees to provoke Cassio into discrediting himself.
- Iago informs the audience of further motives for revenge.

By removing the Turkish threat, Shakespeare can now focus the narrative solely on the personal conflicts. The storm may also be read as a **symbol** for the passions at play and, given its obscuring nature (the characters on land can't see whose ship is landing), it might also represent the inability of Othello to see the truth of his later predicament.

Notice how the sequencing of the arrival of the characters allows the audience to witness Cassio's regard for Othello and Desdemona, and Desdemona's concern for the late arrival of her husband's ship. When Othello does arrive, the audience also observes the great regard he has for his wife – she is his first concern. This scene also provides Iago with some ideas for his revenge plot and, in the closing soliloquy, further insight into Iago's scheming.

aside lines spoken directly by a character to the audience, which other onstage characters don't hear

symbol an object that represents someone or something else

Activity 4

Iago's lines **'That Cassio loves her, I do well believe't... Knavery's plain face is never seen till us'd'** provide several revelations to the audience. Re-read the soliloquy and compose a spider diagram that notes:

- how he feels towards Desdemona
- why he feels aggrieved towards Othello and what he plans to do
- how he will use Cassio in his plot.

Act 2, Scene 2

In this very brief scene, a Herald announces a public holiday to celebrate the destruction of the Turkish fleet and Othello's marriage. The audience is well aware that the festivities are a precursor to the problems that are about to unfold. The evening bonfires and revelry perhaps provide a structural link to Iago's earlier address to Hell and night to **'bring this monstrous birth to the world's light'** (*Act 1, Scene 3*), for it is after this that the tragedy gathers pace.

Act 2, Scene 3

This is where Iago's plans begin to take effect. The scene has shifted again, this time to outside the guard room in the fortress. It takes place on the evening of the public holiday celebrations.

- Othello leaves Cassio and Iago in charge of maintaining order while he goes to consummate his marriage. Iago gets Cassio drunk and, when Cassio sets out to perform his duty, Iago tells Montano that Cassio has a drink problem.
- Offstage, as per Iago's instructions, Roderigo antagonizes Cassio. The pair enter the stage and Cassio strikes Roderigo. Montano, trying to part the combatants, finds himself in a fight with Cassio.
- Roderigo, again on Iago's instructions, cries 'mutiny' around the town and rings a bell, bringing Othello onstage, having disturbed his wedding night. Iago recounts the events to Othello (pretending reluctance) and Cassio is dismissed.
- Iago and Cassio remain onstage, where Iago suggests Cassio should seek Desdemona's help to get back into Othello's favour, a move that will enable Iago to convince Othello that Desdemona is in love with Cassio.
- Roderigo is next persuaded to remain in Cyprus. Iago decides to use his own wife, Emilia, to persuade Desdemona to favour Cassio.

In addition to advancing the plot, one of the functions of this scene is to convey the extent of Iago's evil nature. The delight he takes in using the honest Desdemona and his plan to exploit his own wife speak volumes about his corrupt actions and morals. The plot also gives an indication of the tricks that Iago will employ to manipulate Othello later in the play.

In performance, this is often a lively spectacle, featuring physical violence, drunkenness, a ringing bell and an enraged Othello. The chaos on stage appears to echo the chaotic passions that drive the characters.

Chaos reigns as Cassio (in the air), Roderigo, Lodovico, Iago and Montano get drunk, Lyric Hammersmith, 2015

Key quotation

So will I turn her virtue into pitch,
And out of her own goodness make the net
That shall enmesh them all.
(Iago)

Activity 5

Create a spider diagram or make notes on the content of Iago's soliloquy beginning, 'And what's he then that says I play the villain'. What attitudes towards the other characters does he reveal, particularly towards Desdemona?

Act 3, Scene 1

This scene takes place outside Desdemona's bedchamber.

- Cassio has paid musicians but Othello has sent a clown to dismiss them.
- Iago enters and agrees to distract Othello so Cassio can speak with Desdemona.
- Emilia enters, telling Cassio that Desdemona has already started to plead Cassio's case for reinstatement.

It is important to note here that Iago is not only manipulating Cassio, whose meeting with Desdemona will be used against him, but also Emilia.

The dialogue at the beginning of the scene contains a lot of **bawdy humour**, making **puns** related to genitalia, offering some **comic relief** in the light of the previous scene. Note how Cassio's gratitude is expressed in the heavily ironic words he offers to Iago: **'I never knew a Florentine more kind and honest'**.

> **bawdy humour** comedy based on sexual or indecent content
>
> **comic relief** an event or dialogue in a scene that releases tension through humour
>
> **pun** a double meaning; humour based on wordplay

Act 3, Scene 2

This is a very brief scene set at Othello's headquarters, where Othello sends letters to Venice and then inspects the fortifications. It is probable that while Othello is doing this, Cassio speaks to Desdemona. As Othello earnestly goes about his military business, his domestic life is being disrupted.

Act 3, Scene 3

This scene is central in the sense that it occurs at the heart of the play, but it is also the point where Iago's scheming comes together.

- Desdemona and Emilia reassure Cassio that Othello will soon reinstate him.
- Othello and Iago enter, at which point Cassio leaves. Iago later exploits this hasty departure, insinuating that Cassio has been playing false with Desdemona.
- Desdemona enters and urges her husband to look favourably on Cassio. He wants to discuss it later. Desdemona exits.
- Iago now exploits Othello, while pretending to be supportive. Iago's machinations result in Othello being plagued with doubts about his wife.
- Desdemona enters, dropping a handkerchief that was Othello's first gift to her. Iago comes into possession of it via his wife and plans to plant it at Cassio's lodgings.
- Othello re-enters, fixating on his wife's supposed treachery, yet still uncertain. Iago concocts stories about Cassio to convince Othello.
- Iago agrees to kill Cassio, which will result in Iago becoming lieutenant, and Othello plans the demise of his wife.

> **Key quotation**
>
> Damn her, lewd minx! O, damn her, damn her!
> Come, go with me apart. I will withdraw
> To furnish me with some swift means of death
> For the fair devil.
> *(Othello)*

The length of Desdemona's speech to her husband regarding Cassio raises Othello's suspicion and, once she exits from this scene for the first time, Iago capitalizes on these doubts. Notice how, upon her next entrance, Othello's attitude towards her has changed. The dramatic **motif** of the handkerchief is a useful device, not only in helping Iago's plan to come to fruition, but also in what it reveals about Emilia and Iago's relationship: Emilia acknowledges that '**My wayward husband hath a hundred times/Woo'd me to steal it**'. He later snatches it from her.

Iago's observations before Othello returns to the stage have the function of telling the audience how the handkerchief will be used. The lengthy dialogue between Iago and Othello ('**Excellent wretch… Look where she comes**' and '**Ha, ha, false to me!**'… '**I am your own for ever**') will repay close analysis in the way it reveals Iago's skilful, flexible and manipulative skills and Othello's naivety, jealousy and passions.

By the end of this scene, sometimes referred to as the 'temptation scene', there has been lots of dramatic spectacle: the rapid exit of Cassio, the tension between Othello and Desdemona, the contrary emotions of Othello, the interplay between the **protagonist** and antagonist (often played in a physical way), the motif of the handkerchief, Iago and Emilia's snappiness, the kneeling Othello's anguish, and the decisions that lead to murder and suicide.

> **metaphor** a figure of speech describing a person or thing by comparing them with something that is not literally applicable
>
> **motif** a physical or **metaphorical** item that recurs in a text, taking on a range of meanings
>
> **protagonist** the central character, sometimes (but not always) a heroic figure

> **Activity 6**
>
> Explore the two key segments of dialogue between Iago and Othello: '**Excellent wretch… Look here she comes**' and '**Ha, ha, false to me!**'… '**I am your own for ever**'.
>
> **a)** Note down the main points of the discussion.
>
> **b)** What are the stages in Iago's manipulation of Othello?
>
> **c)** How does Iago lead Othello to wish death upon Cassio and Desdemona? Find the key words he uses.

Act 3, Scene 4

Following what is probably the most important scene in the play, this scene, set outside Othello's lodgings, begins with some comic relief before further disintegration of Othello's relationship with Desdemona occurs.

- Desdemona, seeking Cassio, encounters a clown and has a frustrating pun-based conversation.

- Desdemona worries about the lost handkerchief. Othello enters the stage and they exchange pleasantries but, when she reminds him of Cassio's suit (entreaty/request), his mood changes.

- Othello enquires about the handkerchief. Desdemona lies, saying she still has it. Othello insists that it has familial and magical significance. He storms off stage when she fails to produce it.

- Iago and Cassio arrive. Iago then exits to find out the cause of Othello's rage. Desdemona and Emilia exit.

- Bianca, Cassio's mistress, arrives and wants to know why he has been avoiding her. He produces the handkerchief, which angers her because she thinks it belongs to another woman. He dismisses her concerns, saying he will see her soon.

Although the dialogue with the Clown is light-hearted, it also parallels the previous scene's focus on the confusions of language. Desdemona fails to communicate clearly with the Clown in the same way that confusion, deceit and misinformation cause problems elsewhere.

You may notice that Emilia, who does know what has happened to the handkerchief, keeps quiet about it here. Her function in this scene is partly to offer comment on the action. Her observation that jealousy is 'a monster / Begot upon itself, born on itself' *(Act 3, Scene 4)* echoes Othello's line in the previous scene describing 'the green-eyed monster' *(Act 3, Scene 3)*.

Sympathy in this scene seems to lie with Desdemona, who appears to be a victim of both Iago and now her husband. Her lie is understandable and Othello's manner perhaps makes him less sympathetic.

The dialogue between Bianca and Cassio offers a parallel to the main action. Their dispute is also over jealousy and Cassio's words remind us that, like Desdemona, Bianca simply has to accept her lover's judgement and actions.

Activity 7

Act 3 features many examples of confusion and misunderstanding between the characters. Look back over the play so far and list examples from the first three acts where characters fail to see the true meaning of situations and actions.

Act 4, Scene 1

This is another dramatic scene in which Othello's jealousy has physical manifestations.

- Iago suggests to Othello that his wife has slept with Cassio. Othello faints. Cassio arrives but is sent away by Iago.

- Othello recovers and is told by Iago to hide a distance away. This means that when Cassio re-enters, Othello can see his actions but not quite hear his words. Cassio talks about Bianca in an offhand way and Othello assumes he's referring to Desdemona.

- Bianca enters and angrily produces the handkerchief, which Othello takes as proof of Desdemona's infidelity. Cassio and Bianca exit.

- Othello is distraught. Iago says he will murder Cassio.

- Desdemona and Lodovico enter. Othello is to return to Venice and Cassio to become governor of Cyprus. Othello wrongly assumes his wife is happy because Cassio has been promoted. Othello strikes his wife.

- Othello exits and Iago suggests to Lodovico that Othello has committed worse acts. Lodovico is 'sorry that I am deceiv'd in him'.

'I have not deserv'd this': the audience sees Desdemona (Natalia Tena) as the undeserving victim of Othello's (Patrice Naiambana) abuse, Warwick Arts Centre, 2009

Othello's physical reactions to his wife's supposed infidelity are a significant part of the onstage spectacle. The dramatic faint suggests the depth of anguish Othello feels and, structurally, allows space for Iago to confess his joy and to arrange Cassio's exit and reappearance. When Othello strikes Desdemona, his reputation is ruined and the sympathy we feel for her increases further. Othello is on the cusp of madness and the fact that Lodovico arrives to witness the violence is significant.

The confusion and misunderstanding that occur elsewhere in the play are evident here – the asides from **'Look how he laughs already!'** to **'By heaven, that should be my handkerchief!'** help the audience see Othello's mistaken thought processes. The disjointed nature of his lines reveals his torment and contrast noticeably with Iago's control. The drama in this scene also arises from Othello's position, which renders him unable to hear what Cassio is saying. The audience, however, like Iago, is fully aware of the situation and can see how the characters are being manipulated.

> **Key quotation**
>
> Ay, let her rot and perish, and be damned for tonight, for she shall not live. No, my heart is turned to stone.
> *(Othello)*

Act 4, Scene 2

Emotions run high in this scene, which again contains instances of characters misunderstanding each other.

- Othello quizzes Emilia about Desdemona and Cassio. Emilia defends Desdemona, then fetches her, before exiting to leave the unhappy couple alone.
- The dialogue between Othello and his wife is one of tears, accusation, despair, defence and questions. He accuses her of being an **'Impudent strumpet!'**
- Emilia re-enters, trying to comfort a shocked Desdemona, who asks Emilia to make her bed up with her wedding bedsheets.
- Iago enters, playing a gallant role and offering solace to Desdemona. Emilia's support is more forthright. She suspects someone has been slandering Desdemona.
- Desdemona and Emilia exit. Roderigo enters, about to return home. Iago persuades him to stay in Cyprus and involves him in the plot to kill Cassio.

Othello hurls a range of insults at Desdemona, the repetition of which conveys the depth of his anger. She is given much less dialogue in this scene, perhaps indicating her shock at her husband's accusations.

Like the handkerchief, the bedsheets requested by Desdemona have symbolic qualities. They represent the matrimonial consummation and suggest Desdemona's attempt to regain her husband's loyalty (see Symbolism, page 68).

Once again, **dramatic irony** is evident in Emilia's assertion that some villain – **'Some busy and insinuating rogue'** – has played foul. Her husband's dismissal of this idea perhaps elicits a gasp from the audience. The terms Emilia applies to this villain are worth close investigation.

> **dramatic irony** where the audience possesses more knowledge than the characters about events unfolding on stage

Activity 8

Names and terms applied to characters are often significant. They reveal a lot about attitudes and the ways in which characters are perceived.

In this scene, Desdemona has several names applied to her. Make a list of these and then compare them to the way she is addressed (and by whom) in Act 1, Scene 2; Act 1, Scene 3; Act 2, Scene 1; Act 3, Scene 1; Act 3, Scene 3.

Act 4, Scene 3

Desdemona's bedchamber is the setting for this scene.

- Lodovico wishes Desdemona goodnight and Othello commands her to **'Get you to bed on th'instant'**, after which they exit, leaving Desdemona and Emilia alone for the remainder of the scene.

- Emilia and Desdemona discuss her plight. Desdemona, perhaps naively, passively accepts her situation. She tells a tale of her mother's tragic maid Barbary and sings the 'willow song'.

- The women converse about infidelity, with Emilia acknowledging that women have betrayed men and that husbands have faults.

There is a division in the attitudes of the women towards Othello and marriage in general. Desdemona, as befits an innocent victim, takes a romantic view. Emilia, in contrast, thinks that there are circumstances in which infidelity might be acceptable, asking **'who would not make her husband a cuckold, to make him a monarch?'** Interestingly, Emilia, who appears genuinely supportive here, still hasn't revealed what she knows about the handkerchief.

Activity 9

Emilia's thoughts on men, women and fidelity make interesting reading. Explore her argument beginning, **'Yes, a dozen…'**.

a) Note down your responses to each of her views.

b) Write a paragraph considering whether this speech alters your view of Emilia.

Act 5, Scene 1

The final act begins with a violent scene, which reveals the depth of Iago's evil nature. The bloodshed in the scene aids the drama and prepares the audience for the deaths in the following scene.

- Roderigo prepares to ambush Cassio, assured that Iago will support him. He does wound Cassio, who wounds him in return. Iago stabs Cassio.

- Othello, hearing the voices, appears at a balcony and, assuming Cassio is dying, reminds himself to murder Desdemona.

- Lodovico and Gratiano enter, bewildered by events. Iago enters and plays the helper. While Cassio is being assisted, Iago kills Roderigo.
- Bianca enters, aghast at Cassio's injury. Iago seizes the chance to blame her for colluding in the attack, claiming, '**I do suspect this trash / To be a party in this injury**'.
- Roderigo's body is carried out and Emilia enters. Following her husband, she rounds on Bianca. As Cassio is taken away to be tended, Iago admits uncertainty about what might happen next, noting, '**This is the night / That either makes me, or fordoes me quite**'.

The night-time setting of this scene perhaps suggests the metaphorical darkness of Iago and the brutality that occurs. Yet it also has the practical purpose of disguising actions, allowing Iago to attack both Roderigo and Cassio. It also gives rise to Othello's misunderstanding about Cassio, which ironically prompts him to get on with his revenge.

The scene is rich in dramatic spectacle: the physicality of the scene, Iago's exits and entrances, his appearance with a light, the dressing of a wound, the removal of bodies and the forthright words of Emilia create a sense of drama.

Key quotation

> Strumpet, I come!
> Forth of my heart those charms, thine eyes, are blotted;
> Thy bed, lust-stain'd, shall with lust's blood be spotted.
> (Othello)

Act 5, Scene 2

The play has been building to this tragic moment and, before the curtain falls, both Desdemona and Othello die, and the truth about Iago emerges.

- Desdemona is sleeping in bed when Othello enters. He reflects on what he is about to do and kisses her. She wakes and, during the course of the dialogue, realizes that he is going to kill her.
- Othello smothers Desdemona. Emilia enters, revealing that Cassio is alive. Desdemona briefly recovers and Emilia learns what Othello has done. Desdemona dies. Emilia confronts Othello and declares Iago a liar.
- Emilia's cries bring Montano, Gratiano and Iago onstage. Emilia confronts her husband, who admits his actions. Othello, realizing his grave error, falls on the bed.
- Emilia defends Desdemona's honour and refuses to be silent. Iago stabs her and she dies. Iago is restrained. Othello wounds Iago.
- Letters found in Roderigo's pocket confirm the truth of the situation. Othello stabs himself, dying on the bed. Iago remains silent. He is then taken away and Lodovico promises to report these events.

The fervour of the previous scene contrasts with the relatively quiet opening of this one. Othello's soliloquy, delivered in the bedroom by candlelight, is marked by his contrary emotions and actions – **'O balmy breath, that doth almost persuade/ Justice to break her sword!'** He kisses Desdemona but plans to kill her. His lines are by turns poetic and exclamatory.

The enclosed nature of the room and the significance of the bed – a place of love, privacy, imagined betrayal and death – adds to the tension. The bed itself, where Desdemona's corpse lies during the second half of the scene, is the place where Emilia and Othello's bodies rest too. The drama is aided by the violence, Emilia's forthright accusations and her desire to enter the locked door, the drawing back of the bed curtains and, of course, murder.

Othello's misinterpretation of Desdemona's line, **'Alas, he is betray'd, and I undone'** gives him a reason to presume her guilt. However, the endings of narratives are usually places where misunderstandings are cleared up and revelation occurs. In this scene, Othello learns that Cassio lives and that his wife was innocent. Emilia faces what she may have already suspected – her husband's villainy. The play ends conventionally for a tragedy, with the death of the protagonist.

Key quotation

Wash me in steep-down gulfs of liquid fire!
O Desdemon! Dead Desdemon! Dead! O! O!
(Othello)

Activity 10

In his final soliloquy, Othello offers a view of himself by which he would like to be remembered. Read this speech carefully and consider:

- how he describes his deeds
- how he describes Desdemona
- whether you regard this as a fair account of his actions in the play.

Tips for assessment

Once you have read *Othello*, read it again in conjunction with the notes in this section. Any parts of the play with which you are less confident need to be mastered.

Knowing the text really well allows you the freedom to select the very best quotations and references to explain the point you are making. Students who are unsure of parts of the text often rely on the scenes they know best even if they are not really relevant to the question they are being asked. This means their answer will not be as good as it could be.

Structure

Writing about the structure of a text is different from focusing simply on the events of the play. When you explore the plot, you are considering the events that happen. When you think about structure, you are thinking about the order and manner in which those events are revealed to the audience.

You will have noticed some basic structural aspects already, such as the division of the play into acts and scenes, and the way in which the first act is set in Venice and the remainder of the play is in Cyprus. As well as thinking about the way the story is arranged at the level of the whole plot, it is also useful to analyse the way action is structured *within* scenes.

The overall structure

Dramatic plot centres on conflict and disorder. *Othello* explores the collapse of order and its subsequent restoration. The challenge to order takes several forms, both personal and political.

In tragedy, an initial disorder leads to further problems. This disruption signals the start of the protagonist's problems and the acts that follow intensify the conflict.

You will have noticed that the play opens after several key events have happened. The **backstory** of Cassio's promotion, Othello's marriage and Iago's exploitation of Roderigo have all occurred. The play's dramatic focus is the way in which Iago takes his revenge upon Othello, manipulating others as he does so.

The structure of drama usually moves through **complication** to **catastrophe** to **resolution**. In **dramatic tragedy**, there is usually a restoration of order, brought about by the death of the protagonist. The closing scene often shows the community response to the tragedy: Lodovico's lines at the end of the play suggest that the story of Othello will reach the wider world. There is often a sense of optimism that villains are punished and a more settled world can begin.

> **Key quotation**
>
> Myself will straight aboard, and to the state
> This heavy act with heavy heart relate.
> (*Lodovico, Act 5, Scene 2*)

backstory events that have happened before the play begins

catastrophe the climactic moment, usually the darkest moment in the play

complication an event that intensifies an existing conflict

dramatic tragedy a play that shows the downfall and suffering of the protagonist, usually a person of great stature

resolution the final part of the story, in which a problem is resolved

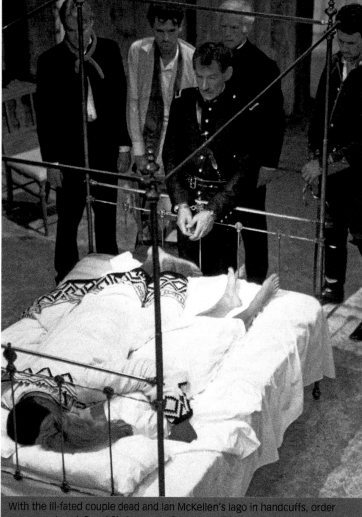

With the ill-fated couple dead and Ian McKellen's Iago in handcuffs, order seems restored, Royal Shakespeare Company, 1989

 Activity 11

Using the plot summaries in the first part of this chapter, explore the disruptions that occur in the structure of the story. Identify:

- the initial problem(s) in the early scenes
- where the complications occur
- what leads to the catastrophe
- which events bring about the resolution.

Using characters as structural devices

Shakespeare uses his characters for structural purposes: their actions set up problems and conflicts, and they occupy a range of functions in the narrative.

A key structural choice is the way in which the audience is prepared for the introduction of the protagonist Othello into the story. Shakespeare structures the opening of the play so that we hear about Othello from other characters, before we meet him. In Act 1, Scene 2, Othello appears on stage for the first time, and the audience have an opportunity to observe his actions and words in the light of Iago's earlier comments. Part of the drama centres upon the visual spectacle of Othello surrounded by angry white faces.

At the end of Act 1, Scene 3, the character of Brabantio foreshadows events to come. He warns Othello of Desdemona's ability to deceive, something which returns to Othello's mind later. The audience also recognizes the danger in Iago's accompanying Desdemona to Cyprus. Iago's comment that Othello **'thinks men honest that but seem to be so'** spells danger *(Act 1, Scene 3)*. By establishing doubts about Desdemona at an early stage in the structure, Shakespeare prepares the audience for events later in the narrative.

When the setting moves to Cyprus at the start of Act 2, Shakespeare structures the arrivals of the characters to allow the audience to observe their attitudes towards each other. This sequencing invites the audience to witness Cassio's regard for Othello and Desdemona, and Desdemona's concern for the late arrival of her husband's ship. When he does arrive, Othello's great regard for his wife is evident – she is his first concern. Iago's soliloquy offers insight into his devious plans.

The placement of the audience

The placement of the audience in a position of privileged knowledge is crucial to the play's success. The centre of the play – Act 3, Scene 3, which is often referred to as 'the temptation scene' – is structured to allow the audience to see how Iago's scheming operates. Dramatic irony features heavily in this scene, with the audience fully aware of the actual truth during Desdemona's observation about Iago: **'that's an honest fellow'** *(Act 3, Scene 3)*.

Shakespeare positions the audience so they, rather than the characters, know the web Iago is spinning and can only watch as the characters obliviously head for tragedy. We can see how Othello is used and how Desdemona's innocent words **'I'll intermingle every thing he does / With Cassio's suit'** take on a horribly ironic meaning *(Act 3, Scene 3)*.

The exits and entrances in Act 3, Scene 3 are significant. It is important that Othello enters to witness the discussion between Desdemona, Emilia and Cassio. The latter's rapid exit prompts the manipulative Iago to observe knowingly, **'Ha! I like not that'**. He then proceeds to use this innocent exit against Cassio.

Parallels

Structural parallels are also used to reinforce some of the key ideas in the play. Although the dialogue with the Clown in Act 3, Scene 4 is light-hearted, it also parallels the previous scene's focus on the confusions of language. Desdemona fails to communicate clearly with the Clown, in the same way that deceit and misinformation cause problems elsewhere. The dialogue between Bianca and Cassio in this scene also offer a parallel to the main action. Their dispute is also over jealousy and Cassio's dismissive words remind us that, like Desdemona, Bianca is a woman who simply has to accept her lover's judgement and actions. These parallels emphasize the **themes** of deceit and jealousy within the play.

Contrast and tension

Contrast is used throughout the play: the perception of Othello against his true character, the lingering suspicion of Brabantio against the approval of the Duke for Desdemona's actions, and, of course, the dual personality of Iago. In Act 4, Scene 3, the use of contrast is evident in Lodovico's respectful farewell to Desdemona, which sharply contrasts with Othello's commands. The manner in which Othello addresses his wife here is starkly different from the deferential way he greets his **'fair warrior'** when he arrives in Cyprus in Act 2, Scene 1. These contrasting verbal exchanges are useful structural markers that things are going badly for Desdemona.

Shakespeare's manipulation of tension is a key structural feature. For example, in Act 4, Scene 2, the tension in the scene builds from Othello's alternating emotions of love and jealous hatred towards his wife. The images in his speech beginning **'Had it pleas'd heaven...'** reflect these contrary feelings – she is a **'weed, / Who art so lovely fair and smell'st so sweet'**. Roderigo's involvement in Act 4, Scene 2 – and Iago's skilful manipulation of him – have a structural significance too, bringing together the two strands of the plot.

This part of the scene is invested with emotion and drama: Roderigo's dismay at being **'fopped'** by Iago and his threat to **'make myself known to Desdemona'** offer a possible crisis that might disrupt Iago's schemes. The tension doesn't abate with the death of Roderigo but continues through the **falling action** of the play.

Shakespeare structures the final scene so that Desdemona wakes before Othello attempts to kill her. The scene gives way to dialogue, so we can see how Othello continues in his misplaced assumptions in spite of Desdemona's pleas, which also serves to increase the tension as the audience waits to see if she can persuade him against his course of action.

Tension leads to climactic moments and Desdemona's fate (the main source of tension) is the high point of the story. The revelation (to the characters) of Iago's villainy and Othello's suicide bring a release of tension. Tragedies conventionally end with a sense that conflict has been resolved and Lodovico's promise to retell the events brings a sense that order is being restored.

Desdemona (Rebecca Johnson) cannot agree to '... confess thee freely of thy sin' or persuade Othello (Nicholas Monu) she is innocent, Theatre Unlimited, 2002

Writing about structure

Exploring the larger structural features of a story, such as where and how the action starts, how the resolution of the play is brought about and, crucially, when the characters – and audience – discover key information, will help you to see the way in which Shakespeare has shaped the narrative.

Smaller structural aspects such as dramatic irony, **symbolism**, **imagery**, contrast and dialogue will also allow you to demonstrate your understanding of the play at a more analytical level. The ability to analyse the structural features of a text will give your answers much more depth and quality.

falling action sequence of events after the climax but before the resolution

imagery the use of visual or other vivid language to convey ideas

symbolism the use of an object that represents someone or something else

theme an idea that recurs throughout a story

Studying the context of a piece of literature means thinking about the surrounding beliefs and cultural ideas that existed when the work was written. You must also consider how your own personal contexts in the world you live in affect how you might read and interpret a play. In many ways, when deciding on how you view *Othello*, the contexts of reception (the point where you personally 'receive' or experience the play) are as important as the context in which it was written.

Literary source of the play

Today, literary works are expected to be original. In Shakespeare's time, writers usually adapted existing stories.

Many English writers, including Shakespeare, looked to Italy for their inspiration. The main source for *Othello* is a story from a 1566 collection of tales complied by Giovanni Giraldi called *Gli Hecatommithi*. Giovanni Giraldi (1504–1573) was also named Cinthio, hence the story that Shakespeare bases *Othello* on is usually known as 'Cinthio's Story' or 'Disdemona and the Moor'. The collection was not translated into English until long after Shakespeare's death, but it's likely that he read it in translation or heard the story retold.

Cinthio's Story

The British Library gives a condensed version of Giraldi's tale, reproduced here:

In Cinthio's story, the virtuous and beautiful Disdemona is the only character to be given a name. Against the advice of her relatives, she marries the gallant Moor, not through lust but for love of his valour. In recognition of his loyal service, the Moor is made commander of the Venetian forces in Cyprus. He sails there with Disdemona, as well as the deceptive Ensign, the Ensign's young wife (Shakespeare's Emilia) and a Corporal (Shakespeare's Cassio).

The Ensign falls in love with Disdemona and, stung by her rejection, plots to convince the Moor that she has been unfaithful with the Corporal. When the Corporal is stripped of his rank for wounding another soldier, Disdemona appeals to her husband on his behalf, and the Ensign seizes his chance to accuse them of an adulterous affair.

The Moor demands 'ocular proof' […]. So the Ensign shows him a handkerchief stolen from Disdemona and planted in the Corporal's house. The Ensign is then bribed by the Moor to kill the Corporal, but only wounds him […]. Together they also scheme to murder Disdemona […].

After her death, the Moor and Ensign turn against each other. The Moor is tortured, exiled and killed by Disdemona's relatives. The Ensign, continuing his villainy, is finally imprisoned for another crime and dies as a result of torture.

Activity 1

Make a list of the similarities and differences between the actions and events involving Desdemona in *Othello* and Disdemona in Cinthio's Story.

Shakespeare's version

The full version of Cinthio's Story (which you can find online) is worth comparing for the light it sheds on what Shakespeare's intentions may have been when he adapted it.

Shakespeare's version offers a different slant on the characters' actions and motivations.

Here are some other significant differences in Shakespeare's play:

- The play's title directs the focus on the Moor, who is named Othello.
- Other characters are given names, not just Desdemona.
- The characters of Brabantio and Roderigo are introduced.
- Iago's motives are centred on rivalry over status, not sexual jealousy.
- Iago's wife appears to be unaware of her husband's actions until much later in the play.
- Iago explicitly states his hatred of Othello – there is a rift between them.
- Othello kills his wife unaided and in their bedchamber.
- Othello takes his own life, rather than being murdered.

Activity 2

What effect is created by Shakespeare's adaptation of the original tale? Take each of the points listed above and consider what it adds to the story.

Race

Several references are made to race in the play. It's probable that when the play was written, the term 'Moor' was used in a general sense to mean anyone who was dark skinned. In more specific terms, 'Moor' refers to Muslims, who had conquered and settled in Spain but originated from Morocco. Until the 1500s, these Muslim settlers continued to practise their religion until it was banned in Spain, at which point they were obliged to convert to Christianity.

Under Elizabeth I's reign, Moors were viewed as a threat and the monarch ordered them to be deported on the grounds that they were draining the country's resources. It's likely therefore that the original audiences would have arrived at the play, just like a modern audience, with an understanding of the prevailing attitudes to immigrants. Interestingly, Shakespeare shows us the Duke's more liberal attitude to Othello in Act 1, Scene 3, appreciating his worth to Venice regardless of Brabantio's concerns.

Shakespeare's decision to refocus the story on Othello is fairly novel but not unusual for the time in which it was written. Some plays of the period featured minor Turk or Moorish characters, often dressed in turbans, and played up to familiar stereotypes of exoticism. Representations of more central characters who are Moors or Turks can be found in other literature of the time, including Shakespeare's *Titus Andronicus* and *The Merchant of Venice*.

In comparison to the traits of those characters listed above, Othello seems to possess nobility and a philosophical quality alongside his warrior-like nature. Although ultimately a murderer, it seems in some ways that the play presents a Moor who is unlike the conventional representation of Moors at the time. Othello has some of the temperamental aspects often attributed in literature of the time to his race, but Shakespeare presents a less brutal, although certainly flawed, hero.

Stereotypes

Most cultures have a stereotypical image of other racial groups. Given that Shakespeare's original audience would have been predominantly white, it's worth considering the extent to which Othello as a character echoes racial stereotypes that existed when the play was written.

Here are some common (mainly negative) racial stereotypes about, and representations of, black people that the original audience might have recognized. Black people:

- exuded an aura of exoticism and otherness
- were barbaric and had a tendency towards savagery
- were not supposed to marry white people
- communicated a sense of danger
- were driven by sexual desire
- were associated with witchcraft
- were emotionally demonstrative
- were fickle and untrustworthy
- were animalistic and lacked logic and reason
- lacked discipline, were lazy and tended towards criminality.

Paolo Veronese's *The Adoration of the Magi*, painted in the 1570s, shows the perceived exoticism of a black king to Europeans at that time

Activity 3

To what extent do the actions and attitudes in the play reflect the racial stereotypes listed on the previous page? How is Othello, the character, more than a stereotype? Write two paragraphs discussing these questions.

Key quotation

Whether a maid so tender, fair, and happy,
So opposite to marriage that she shunn'd
The wealthy curled darlings of our nation,
Would ever have, t'incur a general mock,
Run from her guardage to the sooty bosom
Of such a thing as thou
(Brabantio, Act 1, Scene 2)

Racial language

Before Othello arrives on stage, he is described in terms that draw attention to his appearance and perceived racial characteristics. It is important to note that the words below are said before the audience sees Othello:

> **Key quotations**
>
> What a full fortune does the thick-lips owe,
> If he can carry it thus!
> *(Roderigo, Act 1, Scene 1)*
>
> Zounds, sir, you're robb'd; for shame, put on your gown;
> Your heart is burst; you have lost half your soul;
> Even now, now, very now, an old black ram
> Is tupping your white ewe. Arise, arise;
> Awake the snorting citizens with the bell,
> Or else the devil will make a grandsire of you.
> *(Iago, Act 1, Scene 1)*
>
> you'll have your daughter covered with a Barbary horse, you'll have your nephews neigh to you, you'll have coursers for cousins, and jennets for germans.
> *(Iago, Act 1, Scene 1)*
>
>   your fair daughter,
> At this odd-even and dull watch o'the night,
> Transported with no worse nor better guard,
> But with a knave of common hire, a gondolier,
> To the gross clasps of a lascivious Moor
> *(Roderigo, Act 1, Scene 1)*

Clearly, Iago and Roderigo exploit some of these prejudices as a way of provoking Brabantio. You will notice that a great deal is made of the concept of a black man sleeping with a white woman, and the possibility of miscegenation (interbreeding of different races), which would have been regarded with horror in some quarters in the society of the time.

Othello's sensuality and sexuality is drawn attention to by Iago, and to an extent the play draws attention to the protagonist's warrior-like qualities. Othello's words, whilst often poetic, make reference to his dominance and passion. His actions – the way in which he changes his opinion of his wife – perhaps suggest the negative stereotype of fickleness and illogicality cited above. However, Shakespeare carefully structures the play's sequence so that when we do meet Othello, we are forced to re-evaluate the descriptions of the protagonist that Iago and Roderigo offer in Act 1, Scene 1.

> **Key quotation**
>
> These Moors are changeable in their wills *(Iago, Act 1, Scene 3)*

Activity 4

Having heard Iago and Roderigo's negative descriptions of Othello in Act 1, Scene 1, the protagonist appears on stage for the first time in Act 1, Scene 2. How does Othello's first speech from '**Let him do his spite...**' to '**But look what lights come yond!**' reinforce or challenge these negative descriptions?

Activity 5

Think about the ways in which you might interpret race in relation to the events of the first act. How far do you agree with the following statements? Make notes on what you agree and disagree with in each one.

A

> The words spoken by Iago, Roderigo and Brabantio about Othello provoke a sort of embarrassed comedy. A white Elizabethan audience would recognize the stereotypes and, while they might be offended by the idea of a mixed-race couple, they secretly find a comic recognition in the descriptions of over-sexualized black men and the paternal horror expressed by Brabantio.

B

> The audience is forced to re-evaluate the easy stereotypes offered in Act 1, Scene 1 and come to view Othello as a much calmer, philosophical and romantic character. There is a conscious attempt to draw attention to the casual racism that exists and to offer a different, more balanced view to that offered by Iago, Roderigo and Brabantio.

C

> Othello's initial words make him appear balanced, confident and logical, but this is undermined by his actions later in the play, which serve to confirm some of the racial stereotypes. By the end of the play, Othello is little more than a cruel, aggressive, unthinking savage.

Place

The events of the play are fictional but are set in representations of real places: their values and attitudes of the twin settings of Venice and Cyprus would have been recognizable to the original audiences. It's likely that the Christian audience would also have been aware of the threat that the Turks posed, given the ascendancy of Islam and the threat offered by Muslims forces since the Crusades. Acts 2–5 are set in Cyprus, which is depicted as an outpost. The Venice depicted in Act 1 appears on the surface to be a much more cosmopolitan place.

Venice

At the time, Venice was often seen as a positive model of government and place of wealth. It was a city state, which followed admirable political arrangements, being governed by an elected assembly led by an elected duke.

> ### Activity 6
>
> Consider the following perceptions of Venice, with which Shakespeare and his audience would have been familiar. Find evidence from the text to support these perceptions:
>
> - a place where citizens were allowed to express their views
> - a city where strong, decisive governance persisted
> - a state where foreigners were integrated and accepted
> - a city of culture and an aesthetically pleasing city
> - a place where pleasure was available
> - a sexually liberated city, where courtesans (high class prostitutes) operated.

The play shows many events and actions that provide positive and negative slants on the city, at times emphasizing its fairness in the Duke's treatment of Othello and in other scenes **foregrounding** less positive qualities. For example, the Venice of *Othello* is a place where:

- money is paid by Roderigo to Iago to secure Desdemona's affections
- Iago admits to bribing influential people to secure the role of lieutenant
- the city is engaged in a foreign war
- Emilia thinks adultery is permissible to further a career
- racism persists and people are manipulated and lied to.

> **foregrounding** making something stand out

Cyprus

Cyprian history is one of invasion. Given its position – an island at the Syrian end of the Mediterranean Sea – it was ideal as an outpost for countries wishing to have a military presence in the area. Consequently, Cyprus was always a colony, controlled by others, and under threat of invasion because of its strategic importance.

Cyprus is the location where the two value systems of West and East meet. In *Othello*, Cyprus signifies a place of disorder: the play itself refers to Cyprus as a 'war-like isle' and many turbulent events in the play happen there, which suggests violence and a lack of control. For instance:

- In Act 2, Iago gets Cassio drunk and dismissed for his involvement in a fight.
- In Act 3, Iago insinuates that Cassio has been playing false with Desdemona and later agrees to kill Cassio.
- In Act 4, Othello faints, Iago says he will murder Cassio and Othello strikes his wife.
- In Act 5, Iago stabs Cassio, and kills Roderigo and Emilia. Othello smothers Desdemona, wounds Iago and then kills himself.

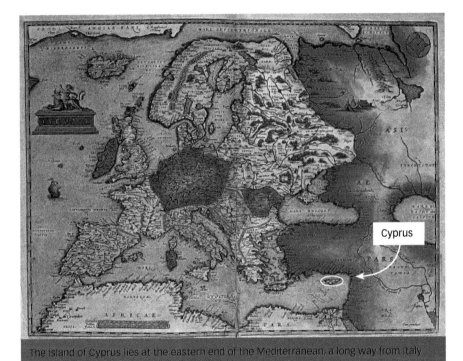

The island of Cyprus lies at the eastern end of the Mediterranean, a long way from Italy

Activity 7

Explore the view that Cyprus can be read as a symbol for the chaotic passions of the characters. Is it too simplistic to say that Venice represents civilization and Cyprus represents disorder? Explain your reasoning, using quotations from the play to support your answer.

Love, desire and the female

Cultural contexts such as those of marriage and companionship are central to the play. *Othello* can be categorized as a story of love, albeit a tragic one. At the heart of the story is a tale of love and jealousy, and so the play deals with emotions that audiences of any era can relate to. Contemporary ideas about love are shown in various ways in the play.

The concept of courtly love, a staple of medieval romantic literature, focused on the female as a highly sought-after, beautiful, refined lady adored by powerful, chivalrous males who competed for her affection. The male lover was a blend of the strong, masculine type and the sensitive, poetic male, who would place his idealized lover on a pedestal.

Desdemona's status as the desired but chaste and faithful female is under attack in the play. Female loyalty and chastity were greatly valued for various reasons, including male pride and economic necessity. The shame and mockery visited upon a male whose wife was unfaithful was a powerful stigma: a cuckold, whose wife was sexually unfaithful to him, was seen as weak and unable to control her. The image of the cuckold – the man forced to wear the horns of a beast as a symbol of ridicule because of his wife's infidelity – finds its expression in art and literature of the time. Infidelity was also an economic concern because it brought into question the paternity of offspring and, in a world where male inheritance was the norm, any suggestion that a male child might be another man's offspring could spell financial and social disaster.

This image of the cuckold and his nagging wife illustrate ideas that pervaded well into the 19th century

---

Key quotation

O, beware, my lord, of jealousy:
It is the green-eyed monster which doth mock
The meat it feeds on.
(Iago, Act 3, Scene 3)

Activity 8

a) Where in the play do you see fears about chastity and cuckoldry? Make a note of these in a table. What do they suggest?

b) To what extent do some of the characters embody the values of courtly love? What might have been Shakespeare's purpose for this?

Female stereotypes

The play offers interesting reflections of the way in which women act and behave, which in part embody some of the cultural beliefs of the period. In the society of the time, women were regarded as inferior to men. The widely held belief in the Great Chain of Being (a medieval system of classification ranking everything from God through to mineral) placed women below men in terms of importance, but above animals. Women were usually expected to obey men and speak when spoken to.

Here are some of the ways in which women were viewed, judged and represented in art, literature and public life at the time the play was written:

- **As a possession of men:** Women's status was determined by their relationship to men as both wives and daughters, and it was expected that women would obey their husbands, a view supported by Church teachings and the Bible. Women were passed, like a possession, from father to husband via marriage.

- **As domestic:** Women were largely seen as less intelligent than men and destined for a life of domesticity. They were allowed little access to education but were expected to be skilled in homemaking, needlecraft and child-rearing. Women of status were expected to avoid the public sphere in spite of their position. Those of lesser status were destined for roles of servitude.

- **As temptresses:** The pervasive image of women as the temptresses of men has its roots in the way Eve is represented in the Bible. She was tempted by the serpent (Satan) and in turn tempted Adam, which links women to evil and danger. An earlier form of this image is that of the Siren in Greek mythology, who could seduce men and lure them to their destruction. Women's physical attractiveness to men was viewed as dangerous as it made men weak, compromising their judgement and thereby affecting the political and social worlds they ruled over.

- **As unreliable:** The opposing associations of men being creatures of reason and women being inconstant, illogical and emotional persisted in Elizabethan times. Women were thought of as driven by mood rather than thought. The medieval image of Dame Fortune, spinning her wheel and determining people's fate by chance is a reflection of female fickleness and unpredictability.

- **As virgins and whores:** The desire of men to possess a valuable, chaste and loyal wife was contrasted with the male desire to find sexual pleasure with morally and sexually loose women. The sexually lively female was a source of attraction but was not considered marriage material. It was considered normal for men to seek sexual fun outside of marriage. For women, such behaviour risked condemnation.

- **As victims and outcasts:** The image of the chaste, unworldly, idealized female often found its expression in victimhood. Such women were represented in literature as potential targets for men, but if their idealized qualities were lacking or they were seduced, punishment (often death) resulted. The shrew or the scold – the nagging, mouthy wife – was particularly despised and could find themselves enclosed in a scold's bridle. Women on the fringe of society, who didn't fit comfortably into the narrow roles available, could be deemed witches.

Key quotation

Awake! What ho, Brabantio! Thieves, thieves!
Look to your house, your daughter, and your bags!
Thieves, thieves!
(Iago, Act 1, Scene 1)

Activity 9

a) Which, if any, of the six stereotypes of women listed above might you place Desdemona, Emilia and Bianca in?

b) Are the females in the play any more than versions of these stereotypes?

Courtesans

As noted in the section on Venice, audiences of the time associated that city with sexual freedom and, in some cases, questionable morality. The women of Venice, as reported in Thomas Coryat's 1611 account of the city, seemed to embody the idea of women being exotic and other-worldly. English readers would have been familiar with the concept of the courtesan (a companion of high-status males), who provided sexual gratification among other things. Courtesans were a kind of high-class prostitute and their existence seemed to reinforce ideas about the freedoms of Venice.

Activity 10

Consider the way in which the relationship between women, sex and finance is shown in the play.

a) How does Iago exploit ideas about Venetian women, and women in general, in his manipulation of Othello and Roderigo?

b) How is Cassio's relationship with Bianca regarded by the other characters in the play? How do you react to it?

Attitudes in the play towards sex are worth considering in relation to the ways in which men and women were expected to behave. For men, adultery and consorting with prostitutes was unproblematic. Female attitudes towards adultery are explored in the differing views of Desdemona and Emilia in Act 4, Scene 3.

Activity 11

Following her recital of the 'Willow Song' in Act 4, Scene 3, Desdemona asks Emilia about the ways in which women regard loyalty to their men. Carefully read the dialogue from **'I have heard it said so…'** to the end of the scene. Then carry out the tasks below.

a) Highlight the key points made by the participants about cuckoldry.

b) Summarize Emilia's argument.

c) Consider what is revealed about Desdemona and Emilia in these lines.

d) Consider your reactions to Emilia and Desdemona's views. How do your own context and values affect your view of Emilia?

Writing about context

Be careful not to deal with context in a generalized way. Although it's possible to talk about the general beliefs held by Elizabethans, avoid making sweeping statements that assume that all Elizabethans were racist or misogynistic, for example. As a comparison, think about all the people you know and consider whether their views can be lumped together as 'what 21st-century people think'.

It is best to couch any points you make about context in tentative terms and let the contextual material arise naturally from the play. Simply expressing some facts about contexts of production will not add much to your writing. Any writing about context should be linked to the events of the play. The material in this chapter has shown how to link contextual ideas to the play. Using these methods in your own writing will help you to handle context effectively.

Othello as a tragedy

One very important context against which *Othello* can be read is that of literary genre. Genre refers to the text type or category a piece of writing can be placed in. By putting a label on a text, readers begin to interpret them – they come to expect certain events and actions to occur.

One way to view *Othello* is as a dramatic tragedy. Like any genre, tragedy has a set of conventions, which a playwright can work within or against (or both).

The term 'tragedy' is commonly used to describe sad events that occur in everyday life but, in literature, tragedy is a stylized representation of suffering with a set of recognizable conventions. Tragedy dramatizes how the actions of characters and the actions of fate bring about disastrous outcomes, usually death.

The first tragedies were written by Greek dramatists such as Euripides and featured the collapse of societies and great people. Shakespeare took some of the conventions of these dramas but also developed them, producing tragic plays such as *King Lear* and *Hamlet*. Both of these texts explore how important people make errors of judgement, or how they are conspired against, and subsequently contribute to their own demise.

In spite of its sombre subject matter, dramatic tragedy brings pleasure to the audience, as well as provoking pity. In watching the succession of dire events, pleasure is derived from the way in which the play unfolds and in the artistic quality of the language. Strong emotions are aroused and it is possible that viewers receive an education of some sort – they are given the opportunity to reflect upon the more difficult aspects of human existence.

Conventions of tragedy

Although there are many different types of tragedy and the genre varies over time, there is a loose set of conventions that comprise literary tragedy. These can include the following:

- a plot that features a central protagonist who appears to have a weakness or flaw that drives their actions
- a protagonist who, either through their own actions or that of fate, suffers and loses their status
- a sense of inevitability about the protagonist's downfall
- a villain or external force that threatens the protagonist
- a protagonist who does things that may be viewed as wrong, yet the audience retains sympathy for the character

- episodes of violence, disorder and suffering
- the death of the protagonist as a way to solve problems set up in the play
- a sense that order is restored at the very end of the play.

Activity 1

Using the list above, explore how far *Othello* adheres to these conventions. Identify where in the play these tragic elements occur.

Political or private tragedy?

Classical tragedy is sometimes thought of as a genre that deals with scenes of political power rather than domestic ones. Shakespearean tragedy is often set in public places associated with powerful people and this is true, in part, for *Othello*. The two geographical settings of the play, Venice and Cyprus, are oppositional. Venice is often shown to be a place of wealth and culture, and perhaps vice too, while Cyprus is represented as an outpost – a place on the edge of Christian influence. It is possible to see Desdemona and Othello as victims of the military and personal honour that pervades the world of Cyprus they find themselves in.

Desdemona (Olivia Vinall) and Othello (Adrian Lester) are totally absorbed in their reunion, surrounded by embarrassed soldiers serving a political regime, Royal Shakespeare Company, 2013

There are also scenes that take place in more private, domestic places. It is worth considering the extent to which the play can be seen as more of a domestic tragedy than a public one. Here is a list of the locations in the play:

1.1 The street outside Brabantio's house

1.2 Othello's lodgings at the Sagittary

1.3 The Duke's council chamber

2.1 Cyprus

2.2 A public place in the town

2.3 Outside the guard room

3.1 Outside Desdemona's bedchamber

3.2 Othello's headquarters

3.3 Othello's lodgings

3.4 The street outside Othello's lodgings

4.1 A street

4.2 Othello's lodgings

4.3 Desdemona's bedchamber

5.1 Outside Bianca's house

5.2 Desdemona's bedchamber

Activity 2

a) Using the list above, explore whether the story is more centred on public or private settings. In which places do the most tragic moments of the story occur?

b) Discuss whether you view *Othello* as a political or a domestic tragedy.

Order and disorder

The structure of most tragedies shows a movement from order to disorder, with a form of order being restored by the end of the play. The early scenes of a play show an ordered world where people know their place and respect the power structures that exist in the world of the play. In *Othello*, the Venetians are trying to maintain order whilst military threat looms. Marriage is also a legal and social way of conferring order and status. Iago's actions serve as a threat to the stability of marriage and also the social and professional relationships between the military figures in the play.

In most tragedies, court scenes are often used to establish the values and order of the society of the play. In such scenes, the audience is shown the deferential way in which important figures are treated, and how the functions and wishes of ruling characters are respected. A key part of the structure of a tragedy is to show an ordered society near the opening of a tragedy so the audience can see how order is destroyed as the play progresses. Iago's manipulative behaviour introduces disorder right from the start of the play but, in Act 1, Scene 3, we glimpse the way in which the Duke's council is law-abiding and tries to maintain order in spite of the wider war and Brabantio's claims against Othello.

> **Key quotation**
>
> if I be left behind
> A moth of peace, and he go to the war,
> The rites for which I love him are bereft me...
> ...Let me go with him.
> *(Desdemona, Act 1, Scene 3)*

> **Activity 3**
>
> Read from **'Why, what's the matter...'** to **'It is most true; true I have married her'** in Act 1, Scene 3. Make notes on how the order of the council is shown in the scene. Look closely at:
>
> - how the characters address each other
> - the effect of Brabantio's outburst
> - the way the Duke controls the interaction
> - the legal and formal words used.

Villains and victims

Tragic villains such as Iago are a significant cause of disorder in tragic texts. They manipulate the hero and bring about his downfall. They can sometimes display qualities that help us to understand their motivation but whether this is the case with Iago is debatable – his machinations seem driven by professional jealousy and there is little to admire in the way he conducts himself. Desdemona, a classic tragic victim, is manipulated by Iago and mistreated by her husband.

In Act 4, Scene 2, Iago addresses Desdemona politely, referring to her as 'madam' and 'fair lady'. It is clear that he is feigning this deference, offering sympathy and telling her **'do not weep'**. He appears concerned for her, asking **'How is't with you?'**, and because the audience knows that this is a deception, our sympathy for Desdemona is increased. The role of Iago as villain seems quite conventional, in the sense that he is the bringer of disorder. His actions bring about the deaths of Othello and Desdemona.

Desdemona's treatment by her deceived husband creates sympathy. Othello calls her 'whore' and 'callet' (a prostitute). The words she uses about herself suggest that she has an air of naivety: in Act 4, Scene 2 she claims **'I am a child to chiding'** and also seems to see her own victimhood: **'It is my wretched fortune'**. Part of Shakespeare's method in Act 4, Scene 2, and in the wider play, is the use of dramatic irony, which increases our sympathy for Desdemona. Because the audience realizes what is happening and she does not, we feel pity for her situation and also realize what lies ahead for her.

Activity 4

Explore how Iago manipulates Desdemona and the situation from **'What is your pleasure, madam?'** to **'How comes this trick upon him'** in Act 4, Scene 2. How is dramatic irony used and what is its effect?

Othello (Hugh Quarshie) allows himself to be manipulated by Iago into accusing Desdemona (Joanna Vanderham), Royal Shakespeare Company, 2015

Aristotle, tragedy and *Othello*

Aristotle (384–322 BCE), a Greek philosopher, scientist and thinker, offered an outline of tragedy in his text *Poetics*. He based his views on the play *Oedipus Rex* by Sophocles. The conventions he identified are regarded as significant, and to an extent, seem to have influenced Shakespeare. Aristotle describes tragedy as a representation of a serious, complete action, which has magnitude (significance and consequence) and arouses pity and fear in the audience, leading to the **catharsis** of these emotions.

Aristotle suggested that tragic protagonists have greatness – of stature or magnitude – that marks them out as special. Othello's position as a highly regarded military man gives him status and the manner in which he conducts himself in front of the Duke in Act 1, Scene 3 suggests a character who is revered. In order for tragedy to arouse feelings of pity, horror and pleasure in the audience, tragic protagonists must have qualities that the audience can relate to. When the scope of the protagonist's suffering is greater than their error, pity results.

Aristotle applied specific terms to the pattern of the protagonist's experiences. He suggested that tragic characters possess a pronounced self-belief, which makes them carry on with their actions in spite of warnings. This sort of pride he termed **hubris**. The protagonist's errors of judgement, or the specific action that leads to the downfall, he called **hamartia**. The moment when the protagonist becomes aware of the magnitude of their error is known as **anagnorisis**. The term **'peripeteia'** describes the moment of catastrophe – the point where the downfall occurs. The audience's emotional response to the events, the shedding of the feelings of pity and terror that build up during the play, is given the term 'catharsis'.

anagnorisis the moment of recognition when the protagonist realizes the significance of their mistakes

catharsis the emotional release felt by the audience; a sense of cleansing

hamartia a mistake made by the protagonist, which leads to their downfall

hubris excessive pride, which leads characters to ignore warnings and presume that they know best

peripeteia a catastrophe undergone by the protagonist; a reversal of fortune

Activity 5

Apply the terms 'hubris', 'hamartia', 'anagnorisis' and 'peripeteia' to the events of *Othello*. Identify where these moments seem particularly apparent.

Othello as a tragic hero

A tragic hero, or tragic protagonist, is often represented as an outsider. They often find themselves pitted against the values of the world they are part of. There is frequently something admirable in their refusal to simply accept the way things are. Tragic heroes usually have a sense of self-worth bordering on arrogance. They are often flawed individuals, beset by qualities such as ambition or jealousy.

Activity 6

Read the following descriptions of tragic heroes. Which of these accurately describe Othello?

A A tragic hero has strongly independent qualities. They handle the problems they're faced with independently and don't appear to trust others' judgements. They seem unwilling to compromise.

B A tragic hero is destroyed by their own mistakes or some flaw in their character. They are also victims of tragic villains, or fate, or both.

C A tragic hero provokes negative responses in the audience. Their actions cause revulsion and their arrogance can be an unattractive quality.

D A tragic hero provokes positive responses in the audience. Their self-belief and grandeur can be heroic, their philosophical manner attractive, and the scale of their suffering a source of sympathy.

The tragic death

Death in tragic plays usually brings closure – the hero's demise brings about an end to suffering. Dramatic tragedy reveals how errors of judgement lead to isolation, suffering and death, but the death is not always seen as deserved. Usually, it provokes pity and there is often a communal lament for the fallen hero.

As in some films, death scenes can be drawn out and accompanied by a soliloquy in which the protagonist offers their thoughts on their own tragedy. The language is often elevated and stylized. Although the manner of death may be gory, the language has a philosophical beauty that continues to reaffirm the hero's intellectual and emotional qualities, in spite of their crimes.

In Act 5, Scene 2, Othello's speech from **'Soft you; a word or two before you go'** to **'And smote him thus'** seems to operate as a kind of eulogy or a verbal suicide note. In it, he explains how he'd like to be thought of. He provides his own account for the purposes of posterity and tries to explain his actions at the very point he is about to kill himself. He claims he'd **'done the state some service'** and acknowledges both his error and Desdemona's virtues in his admission that he **'threw a pearl away'**. He draws attention to his victimhood and refers to himself in the third person, as if he is offering an impartial account.

Activity 7

How accurate do you find Othello's account of his own life and actions? To what extent is it supported, or not, by the events of the play?

In Othello's final speech, he comes to realize his errors of judgement and knows his death is imminent. In tragedy, protagonists realize their fate is inescapable. One of the wider significances of the genre is that life is random and humans are at the mercy of fate or the cruelty of others.

The tragic experience of Othello provokes a range of responses from different audiences. Tragedies, according to Aristotle, have profound effects on viewers. Aristotle's term 'catharsis', to describe an audience's reaction at the end of a tragedy, is derived from medicine and means purgation – and, by extension, the emotional release felt by the audience.

Othello (Ray Fearon) realizes, too late, that he has misjudged Desdemona (Zoe Waites), Royal Shakespeare Company, 2000

Activity 8

What, if any, emotional reaction do you have to events at the end of the play? Consider these possible responses as a starting point:

> We feel sorrow for Othello's death but see the justice of it. The audience learns the lessons of Othello's actions. The main feeling is one of uplift.

> The overriding emotion is one of sympathy. Othello's experiences challenge us emotionally and provoke us to extend our human sympathies. We are better human beings for having witnessed these horrible events.

> Watching tragedy evokes a sense that life is futile: *Othello* shows us that good and bad people die and life is unfair. The random, cruel nature of life is revealed and the dominant feeling is that life is meaningless.

Writing about genre

Relating the play to its genre will help you to get away from simply writing about the events of the play or the actions of the characters. Dealing with *Othello* as part of a wider literary context, that of tragedy, will help you to bring a sharper focus to the points you make.

Studying the genre of tragedy will illuminate your analysis of how Shakespeare uses and plays with conventions of the genre. It makes sense to have a working knowledge of the aspects of the genre that are found in a variety of tragic plays, but also to be alert to when writers challenge your expectations.

It is important to remember that writers don't write to a formula. Although you may be able to see the skeleton of the genre in *Othello*, when writing about the play as a tragedy, avoid the temptation to simply spot tragic elements and say 'and this is tragic'. Try to get beyond the feature and see what meanings emerge. What does Desdemona's death in her bedchamber signify? What is distinctive about Iago's tragic villainy? Could it be regarded as conventional?

Characterization and Roles

Tips for assessment

Some older critical approaches treat characters as if they are real people, and explore the beliefs and psychology of characters, as if they have a choice in what they do and say. While any study of characters needs to start from what is done and said by the characters onstage, it is essential to explore them as *constructs*. The writer – in this case Shakespeare – decides everything in terms of what appears on the page. Writing about characters is insightful when it looks at *how* characters are constructed, rather than just describing their actions.

There is a difference in writing about characters and *characterization*. The latter looks at the choices made by the dramatist and thinks more widely about the character in relation to character type, role and function in the text. Stepping back and thinking about the choices made by the playwright is comparable to watching a film and thinking less about the things the characters do on screen and more about what the director, scriptwriter, make-up artist, etc. decide to show. Drama is, of course, a special kind of text where different productions of plays can lend a different slant to character. Make sure you balance what is on the page with how it might translate onstage.

Othello

Shakespeare deliberately adapts the original source of the story so that Othello, rather than Desdemona, is the central protagonist (see Context). Othello's **character arc** shows a movement, as does the plot, from order to disorder. His opening speech suggests a character who exudes confidence and control, but this gives way to jealousy, chaos and finally death. Othello exhibits many of the conventions of a tragic protagonist. He is destroyed by his inability to see beyond the jealousy he mistakenly feels as a result of Iago's scheming.

The Othello we see in the early scenes is often described as noble. After Brabantio's emotional accusations against him in Act 1, Scene 2, Othello defends himself in a measured way, which leads the Duke (in part) to side with Othello's account. There seems to be a confidence, which, combined with his military rank and his poetic qualities, lends him an air of ease. At the start of the play, Shakespeare draws attention to Othello's civilized qualities and this then allows the audience to see how far Othello falls by the end of the play.

Shakespeare uses the scene in the council chamber to reveal the backstory of Othello and Desdemona's courtship. His speech in Act 1, Scene 3 helps to characterize Othello, not only in terms of what is revealed, but also the manner in which it is presented.

character arc the progress and development of a character during the text

Activity 1

Explore the following extracts from Othello's recollection of his courtship with Desdemona, and then answer the questions that follow.

A From **'Her father lov'd me, oft invited me...'** to **'Of hair-breadth scapes i'th'imminent deadly breach'** *(Act 1, Scene 3)*

B From **'This to hear / Would Desdemona seriously incline...'** to **'Devour up my discourse'** *(Act 1, Scene 3)*

C From **'I did consent, / And often did beguile her of her tears...'** to **'She gave me for my pains a world of sighs'** *(Act 1, Scene 3)*

D **She lov'd me for the dangers I had pass'd, / And I lov'd her that she did pity them.** *(Act 1, Scene 3)*

a) What does Othello say in extract A of his early life?

b) What does Othello say in extracts B and C about how Desdemona reacts?

c) In extract D, how does Othello characterize their love?

You will have noticed in extract A how Shakespeare has Othello draw attention to Brabantio's affection for him and also to his own heroism. Shakespeare employs many echoes of the adventure genre, so Othello represents himself in autobiographical fashion as a man of action: he braves not only man-made conflicts, but also those of chance and fortune. Desdemona is cast in the role of emotionally charged listener, with Shakespeare using words associated with danger and despair, such as 'disastrous', 'tears', 'distressful', 'pains' and 'pity'.

Activity 2

Read the following statements about extracts A–D. How far do you agree with them?

1 Othello's words make him appear pompous, proud and arrogant.

2 Othello's story of himself suggests a noble, heroic character.

3 A clear distinction is made between Othello as a man of action and Desdemona as a passive, domestic female.

4 Desdemona's attraction to Othello is based on his tales of heroism alone.

5 Desdemona seems foolish for falling in love based on the stories he tells.

6 Their love appears to be built on nothing much at all – it's little surprise that things fall apart in Cyprus.

Key quotation

She wish'd she had not heard it, yet she wish'd
That heaven had made her such a man
(Othello, Act 1, Scene 3)

Othello's position in the social and political structure of the story's world is worth considering. As a general he holds military power and clearly commands the Duke's respect. He is also an outsider, being a Moor, and appears to act deferentially to the white senators. Part of his appeal is the contradictions in his status, and that extends to his character. He is clearly a man of action, but also has a poetic, romantic aspect. In Act 2, Scene 1, Shakespeare shows us Othello's arrival in Cyprus, unaware that even as he professes his love for his wife, Iago is planning his downfall.

Activity 3

Read Othello and Desdemona's dialogue in Act 2, Scene 1 from **'Oh, my fair warrior!'** to **'Succeeds in unknown fate'**. Then:

a) Explore the way they address each other.

b) Note down all of the natural and **metaphysical** imagery in Othello's words. What impression is created of Othello?

metaphysical abstract or non-physical

Othello's descent into chaos is shown in such a way that the audience can see how he is being manipulated. The seemingly noble, poetic exterior gives way to something basic and primitive. Othello is jealous, loses control and this is reflected in his thought patterns and the language used in his soliloquies. In Act 3, Scene 3, he believes Desdemona is unfaithful and, as Iago exits, he reflects upon his Ensign and his wife.

Activity 4

In Act 3, Scene 3, read from **'This fellow's of exceeding honesty…'** to **'For others' uses'**, where Othello considers Iago and Desdemona.

a) Explore the way Iago and Desdemona are described and how Shakespeare's use of dramatic irony contributes to the effect here.

b) Underline the natural imagery used. How does it differ from the imagery you identified in Activity 3?

c) Othello begins to be self-critical here. What seem to be his concerns? How does this contrast with the Othello of the first two acts and, in particular, the description of himself that you explored in Activity 1?

Further unravelling of the protagonist occurs later in Act 3, Scene 3. Notice how, once Iago's plans take effect, Othello becomes a more passionate, anguished character. His language becomes exclamatory, overblown and judgemental.

Key quotations

> when I love thee not,
> Chaos is come again.
> *(Othello, Act 3, Scene 3)*

> Avaunt, be gone! Thou hast set me on the rack.
> I swear 'tis better to be much abus'd
> Than but to know't a little.
> *(Othello, Act 3, Scene 3)*

Key quotations

> Arise, black vengeance, from thy hollow cell!
> Yield up, O love, thy crown and hearted throne
> To tyrannous hate! Swell, bosom, with thy fraught,
> For 'tis of aspics' tongues.
> *(Othello, Act 3, Scene 3)*

> Damn her, lewd minx! O, damn her, damn her!
> Come, go with me apart. I will withdraw
> To furnish me with some swift means of death
> For the fair devil. Now art thou my lieutenant.
> *(Othello, Act 3, Scene 3)*

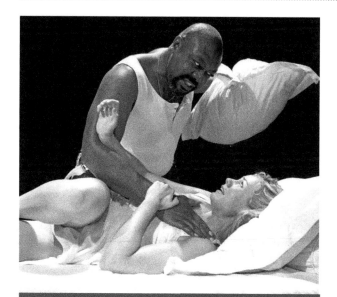

Lenny Henry and Jessica Harris in the lead roles, Northern Broadsides and West Yorkshire Playhouse, 2009

To some readers, Iago's view of Othello as emotional, illogical, easily duped and egocentric is correct. The negative stereotyping of black people you explored in the Context chapter is worth reconsidering at this point. Notice how, as his jealousy takes hold, Othello describes the worth of the handkerchief in a superstitious way:

> **There's magic in the web of it:**
> **A sibyl, that had number'd in the world**
> **The sun to course two hundred compasses,**
> **In her prophetic fury sew'd the work**
> *(Othello, Act 3, Scene 4)*

His primitive explanations seem to call into question the earlier version of Othello as a calm, rational and noble character. The physicality of Othello emerges as the play progresses: the warrior's anger comes to the fore and there are several instances of emotionally driven physical responses in Acts 4 and 5 contained in the stage directions:

- *He falls in a trance (Act 4, Scene 1)*
- *He strikes her (Act 4, Scene 1)*
- *He kisses her (Act 5, Scene 2)*
- *He smothers her (Act 5, Scene 2)*
- *Othello falls on the bed (Act 5, Scene 2)*
- *Othello runs at Iago (Act 5, Scene 2)*
- *He wounds Iago (Act 5, Scene 2)*
- *He stabs himself (Act 5, Scene 2)*

The act of striking his innocent wife in Act 4 is an interesting moment. Shakespeare's inclusion of this action helps to complicate our response to Othello. In one sense, we entirely understand the process of Othello's tragic downfall because we know about Iago's schemes in a way that Othello does not. But the injustices he visits upon his wife may cause you to question where your sympathies lie. The manner in which he talks about and addresses his wife changes noticeably.

In the opening soliloquy of the final scene of the play – '**It is the cause... I'll smell it on the tree**' *(Act 5, Scene 2)* – Shakespeare presents the audience with a calmer Othello, one who attempts to justify his forthcoming murder. The emotion seems to give way to an attempt to confer logic upon his actions.

You will notice how Othello convinces himself of '**the cause**' (her 'crime'), which is adultery. He places himself as a guardian of morality, as if he has the role of deciding what is acceptable conduct. He seems to want a peaceful death for her, as if the virginal image of Desdemona requires preservation. Images of light, nature and death are employed by Shakespeare. The speech – and the action of kissing her – express his conflicting thoughts of torment and love.

This 2004 Royal Shakespeare Company production contrasted Othello and Desdemona, black and white, light and dark

Activity 5

Compare Othello's soliloquy, **'It is the cause... I'll smell it on the tree'** (*Act 5, Scene 2*), with the speech he makes later in the scene when he realizes he has killed Desdemona in error: **'Now, how dost thou look now?... O Desdemon! Dead Desdemon! Dead! O! O!'**

Consider:

- the way he describes his wife
- the nature of the punishments he wishes upon himself
- the imagery used in the speech.

As a tragic protagonist, Othello's fate is held up for inspection and whether you attribute his downfall to internal weakness (his fatal flaw, perhaps) or external forces (Iago, fate, setting) is an important discussion.

Activity 6

Which of these statements do you think adequately describes Othello's downfall?

A	Othello is solely the victim of Iago. As a warrior, he is unused to the ways of Venetian life, and the manner in which he is exploited reveals his innocence of the machinations of the **Machiavellian** Iago. Othello represents all that is good about humanity and the play shows how, in the wrong circumstances, evil flourishes.
B	The roots of Othello's downfall are in his personality. He is an egotist and foolish. The manner in which he is manipulated reveals a man who Iago accurately describes as 'credulous'. His relationship with Desdemona collapses because it is built on slender foundations. Iago merely exposes Othello's flaws.

Machiavellian cunning, scheming and interested in selfish gain; derived from Niccolò Machiavelli's book *The Prince*

51

Iago

Iago, as the obvious villain of the play, may well have the most interesting role in the text. Although the play centres on Othello, it is his malevolent Ensign who has more dialogue and soliloquizes more than you might expect a villain to. Evil and manipulative though he is, Iago is a fascinating character for the audience and is significant in several ways. Not only is he an agent of disorder in the text – the force that helps to bring about the conditions for the protagonist's downfall – he also eludes precise definition, preferring silence to explanation at the end of the play.

As with the protagonist, Shakespeare complicates our response to the villain by revealing recognizable motivations for his crimes, and also by showing Iago's clever improvisation and skilful management of people's thoughts and emotions. It would be difficult to classify Iago as likeable, or even admirable, but there is something seductively watchable in the way he goes about his schemes.

By complicating our response to the characters, Shakespeare makes them more complex. Just as Othello is a character who performs good and evil acts, Iago provokes us to think why we find him an interesting, but unappealing, character.

Some readings of the play propose that Othello represents good and Iago represents evil. You might consider whether this view is too simplistic and whether the characters are more rounded than this. In defying simple categorization, these characters have more depth. You might explore the idea that the terms 'hero', 'villain' and 'victim' are less well defined than first appears: Othello, after all, is a murderer and also a victim of Iago. Whether Iago can possibly be defined as heroic is less likely, but some readings of his character suggest that he strikes a blow for the lower ranks of society against the privileged classes of Venice.

Activity 7

The poet and literary critic Samuel Coleridge said that Iago's malignity is 'motiveless'. In light of this, consider the following extracts in which Iago gives reasons for his actions. Then answer the questions that follow.

- From '**Non-suits my mediators. For 'Certes,' says he...**' to '**Is all his soldiership**' *(Iago, Act 1, Scene 1)*
- From '**Thou art sure of me...**' to '**Let us be conjunctive in our revenge against him.**' *(Iago, Act 1, Scene 3)*
- From '**But for my sport and profit...**' to '**Will do as if for surety**' *(Iago, Act 1, Scene 3)*
- From '**Live Roderigo...**' to '**That makes me ugly**' *(Iago, Act 5, Scene 1)*

a) What are the primary motivations for Iago's scheming?

b) Do you give credence to Iago's explanations?

c) Is Coleridge right in the sense that we can't really ascribe motivation to such actions accurately – and that, in the end, he's just a character who perpetrates bad acts for no real reason?

One structural pattern in the text is the use of soliloquy. Conventionally, the speaker of solo speech is afforded some status in the play – and it's assumed that the words spoken are truthful and represent the speaker's inner thoughts. Villains are usually given asides, and the occasional soliloquy, yet Iago is given the luxury of several soliloquys, some of which are placed at the end of scenes, which appear to elevate his status in the play and draw the audience's attention to his role.

In his speech at the end of Act 1, Scene 3, we see the formulation of Iago's plan. Shakespeare clearly foregrounds the apparent spontaneity of Iago's thoughts, suggesting his flexibility and improvisational skills. Notice Iago's quickness of thought from **'Cassio's a proper man...'** to the end of the scene.

Shakespeare shows us an attractive quality here – speed of thought and a knowledge of human behaviour – even though these skills are put to evil use. A more cynical facet of Iago's character is revealed in his attitude towards women.

Activity 8

Explore Iago's attitudes towards women, including his wife, as revealed in the following extracts. Then answer the questions below.

- From **'Come on, come on...'** to **'You rise to play and go to bed to work'** *(Iago, Act 2, Scene 1)*
- From **'How now? What do you here alone?'** to **'Look, here it is'** *(Iago, Act 3, Scene 3)*

a) How does Iago describe the versions of women in his seemingly light-hearted public utterances to Desdemona?

b) Consider the way he talks to Emilia, his wife, in a private, domestic context.

Iago's manipulative skills abound in the play. During the course of five acts, he:

- extorts money from Roderigo in his pursuit of Desdemona
- arouses Brabantio's anger by revealing his daughter's marriage
- persuades Roderigo to go to Cyprus
- persuades Roderigo that Desdemona loves Cassio
- gets Cassio drunk and informs Othello of his lieutenant's supposed drink problem
- engineers a fight between Roderigo and Cassio
- persuades Cassio to seek Desdemona's help
- uses his own wife to persuade Desdemona to favour Cassio
- suggests to Othello that Cassio is pursuing Desdemona
- secures the handkerchief to use against Desdemona

- pretends to support Othello and protect Cassio, and then agrees to kill Cassio
- suggests that Cassio has slept with Desdemona
- feigns sympathy for Desdemona
- involves Roderigo in a plot to kill Cassio
- suggests he'll support Roderigo, and then kills him.

In examining the above list, it is striking to note how many events Iago controls. His actions drive the plot and within the story's world he controls the fate of many characters. His control is based on keeping his victims isolated from each other, exploiting opportunities when they arise and keeping his schemes hidden. His schemes come to fruition because he prepares traps for his victims and play-acts his role, switching from insinuation to flattery when the situation demands it.

Iago takes pleasure in the unfolding of his plans. After Othello falls into his trance in Act 4, Scene 1, he revels in the effect of his handiwork, exclaiming, '**Work on, / My medicine, work!**'. He moves from underling to someone who commands the general, even to the point where he advises Othello on the best way to kill Desdemona. At the end of Act 4, Scene 1, Iago seems to acknowledge that for all his manipulation, he is reliant in part on luck.

Iago (Rory Kinnear) shares his schemes with the audience, which include manipulating Desdemona and Cassio, behind him on stage, Royal Shakespeare Company, 2013

Key quotations

Do it not with poison: strangle her in her bed, even the bed she hath contaminated. *(Iago, Act 4, Scene 1)*

This is the night
That either makes me, or fordoes me quite *(Iago, Act 5, Scene 1)*

Iago's schemes are eventually revealed by his wife, whom he terms **'Villainous whore'** and **'Filth'**, before he rewards her with death (*Act 5, Scene 2*). He is strangely quiet at the end of the play, refusing to offer an explanation: **'I never will speak word'** *(Act 5, Scene 2)*. His punishment is not death, as seems conventional for a villain in a tragedy, but torture. This may be explained by Venetian justice, which didn't permit the death penalty, but the silence of Iago given his verbosity in the play is unusual. In choosing not to have Iago give an account of his motives or attempt to explain away his crimes – or even seek penance for them – Shakespeare makes the character of Iago more enigmatic. This allows your interpretation of him to be more open to a series of readings.

Activity 9

Consider the following views of Iago. Rank them, starting with the most apt.

- An underling whose lack of status drives his actions
- A cruel, sadistic character who revels in the misery he causes
- A woman-hater who lays the blame for men's misery on women
- An improviser who delights in scheming
- Pure evil – the embodiment of the devil
- A nihilist – a believer in nothing, who simply follows his desires and amoral code
- A victim of his lack of status and the power structures in Venice
- A hero who brings down the privileged and strikes a blow for the less powerful
- A jealous, cowardly character who deserves the torture he will receive
- A man without any real motives

Desdemona

As the primary victim of the play, Desdemona's tragedy appears undeserved. Her death at the hands of the man she loves is a cruel end. She occupies an interesting position in the text: she is perhaps less complex than Iago and Othello, but there is enough ambiguity about her actions and words to make her more than just a straightforward victim.

Desdemona's status gives her some power. She can go to Cyprus with her husband and is clearly a rich Venetian aristocrat but, in many ways, she is powerless. She seems to be a possession of her father and husband, and appears to blame herself for her demise. She is child-like to a degree, younger than her husband, and lacking Emilia's cynicism about relationships. Desdemona appears vulnerable and when she is struck and insulted by her husband, she accepts the domestic abuse in a passive manner, blaming herself for Othello's cruel actions.

Her decision to marry Othello is viewed as controversial in the world of the play, which may well suggest her adoration of him, or naivety, or perhaps wilfulness. The fact that she marries Othello without her father's permission raises the idea – expressed by Brabantio and exploited by Iago – that she is deceptive. It is this ambiguity that is at the root of her tragedy, yet there is no real reason to suggest that she is anything other than faithful. The expectations that are placed upon her position as a female, and the sexual freedoms and fear of cuckoldry that persist in the world of the play, doom her.

Activity 10

Discuss the ways in which Desdemona is referred to in the quotations below from Act 1.

a) What patterns do you notice?

b) What might be said about the way Desdemona is regarded?

c) Which characters do you think are speaking, and at which points in the play?

- Look to your house, your daughter, and your bags!
- an old black ram / Is tupping your white ewe
- you'll have your daughter covered with a Barbary horse
- your fair daughter
- unhappy girl
- I love the gentle Desdemona
- a maid so tender, fair, and happy
- Abus'd her delicate youth
- She is abus'd, stol'n from me
- I won his daughter
- A maid never bold; / Of spirit so still and quiet that her motion / Blush'd at herself
- She has deceiv'd her father
- She must change for youth; when she is sated with his body she will find the error of her choice

Prior to Desdemona's entry in Act 1, Scene 3, the tug of war between Brabantio and Othello sees her described in various ways by the two men. As you saw in the Context chapter, women were (and sometimes still are) defined by their relationships with men. Desdemona is seen as either daughter or wife in the opening scenes. Othello presents her as a young woman besotted with his tales of daring – she has a 'greedy ear'. He also suggests that her role, even as a Venetian of status, is one involving the domestic sphere, whose 'house affairs would draw her thence'. Her father thinks she has been hoodwinked and views her as property, claiming she has been 'stol'n'.

When Desdemona speaks in the council chamber, 'My noble father... Due to the Moor my lord' (Act 1, Scene 3), she doesn't quite seem the naive woman that her father believes her to be. Her speech suggests a sense of deference but also diplomatic skill.

Activity 11

Re-read Desdemona's speech, **'My noble father... Due to the Moor my lord'** *(Act 1, Scene 3)*.

a) What is her argument?

b) How do you respond to the way she presents herself?

c) Is she being genuine or is there a sense that she is cleverly manipulating her father and playing a role here?

Although Desdemona's virtue seems unquestionable, the seeds of her destruction are sown in the words that her father uses at the end of Act 1, Scene 3 when he warns Othello of her potential to deceive. Iago exploits this in Act 3, Scene 3, reminding Othello that **'She did deceive her father, marrying you'** and to some extent we see that Desdemona has the ability to conceal her feelings. In Act 2, she is awaiting her husband's arrival and represses her fears, acknowledging that she conceals her feelings.

It's possible to read Desdemona's tragedy as being one of naivety. When she begs her husband to consider Cassio's suit, she doesn't realize how this may appear to Othello. In Act 5, Scene 2, she utters the words **'Alas, he is betray'd, and I undone'**, without seeing how this might be misinterpreted. Perhaps her inexperience and lack of cynicism is the root of her downfall. Even Iago observes her positive qualities and the potential to corrupt them.

Key quotations

I am not merry, but I do beguile
The thing I am by seeming otherwise –
(Desdemona, Act 2, Scene 1)

She is of so free, so kind, so apt, so blest a disposition, that she holds it a vice in her goodness not to do more than she is requested.
(Iago, Act 2, Scene 3)

Activity 12

What do the following speeches by Desdemona reveal about her worldliness?

A From **'I prithee do so...'** to **'Hath puddled his clear spirit'** *(Act 3, Scene 4)*

B From **'Upon my knees, what doth your speech import?'** to **'But not the words'** *(Act 4, Scene 2)*

C From **'No, as I am a Christian...'** to **'Be not to be a strumpet, I am none'** *(Act 4, Scene 2)*

D From **'It was his bidding...'** to **'We must not now displease him'** *(Act 4, Scene 3)*

Emilia (Rachel Joyce) unmasks the truth to Othello (Ray Fearon) – 'thou hast kill'd the sweetest innocent.' – Royal Shakespeare Company, 2000

Emilia and Bianca

Emilia provides an interesting contrast to Desdemona. Shakespeare presents her as much more than a worldly-wise servant. She appears resigned to the life she leads as Iago's wife, and also to the realities of male and female relationships. She is unaware of her husband's schemes until much later in the play, but is then caught between wishing to protect her husband but also being faithful to Desdemona.

She may be read as another version of the trapped female: a woman who is used by her husband and expected to remain silent when she does realize the truth. It is telling that when she does speak the truth, she perishes. Emilia's dying words see her occupy the role of truth-bringer and her narrative function is in part to bring about the revelation of misunderstandings and treachery. It is Emilia who disabuses Othello of his misconceptions and unmasks her husband's villainy.

> **Key quotations**
>
> You told a lie, an odious damned lie:
> Upon my soul, a lie, a wicked lie!
> She false with Cassio?
> (Emilia, Act 5, Scene 2)
>
> Moor, she was chaste; she lov'd thee, cruel Moor;
> So come my soul to bliss, as I speak true;
> So speaking as I think, I die, I die.
> (Emilia, Act 5, Scene 2)

Activity 13

Consider the following views of Emilia. Which ones do you find most accurate?

- An ignorant wife whose naivety and blind love for her husband brings about her mistress's death
- A put-upon wife, unloved and obliged to protect her dreadful husband
- A realist who understands that morals have to be compromised on occasion
- A force for good who brings about her husband's downfall
- A tragic victim who dies because she tells the truth
- A tragic victim who is trapped between two powerful people

As the third female in the text, Bianca's position reflects another way in which women are perceived. As a courtesan, she is seen as fair game by the characters in the play. Cassio has no qualms about visiting her and views her in opposite ways to how he sees Desdemona. Emilia, in spite of the fact that she realizes the complexities of adult relations, judges Bianca to be a **'strumpet'**.

Activity 14

Othello is a mercenary – he fights wars for money and status, and is valued. Bianca sells her services too but is damned for it. To what extent do you think that the play criticizes the double standards that exist in relation to the ways men and women are perceived? Write two paragraphs to explain your ideas.

Cassio and Roderigo

Cassio, unlike the other characters whose tragic end brings death, lives on at the end of the story and becomes governor, succeeding Othello. Cassio is not burdened with Iago's cynicism and seems to be generally fair and positive in the way he conducts himself. You might wish to consider the extent to which his association with Bianca compromises his integrity, however, in spite of Bianca's love and care for him, he is dismissive of her.

Cassio seems elsewhere to be an echo of the courtly lover, but he is more than just an **archetype**. His gentlemanly manners, combined with his penchant for alcohol and Bianca, suggest a more rounded character. The views of others, and his actions, offer some things for the audience to weigh up.

> **archetype** a typical example; the original model or pattern of something

> **Key quotation**
>
> **I marry her? What! A customer! I prithee, bear some charity to my wit.**
> *(Cassio, Act 4, Scene 1)*

Activity 15

Consider the following facts and views about Cassio. How do you reconcile the different aspects of his persona? Is he anything more than a ladies' man who is used by Iago?

- Iago thinks Cassio is undeserving of the lieutenantship, being inexperienced.
- Cassio's attractiveness is drawn attention to by Iago.
- The manner in which he greets Desdemona might be seen as flirtatious.
- He gets drunk and is provoked into violence.
- He consorts with Bianca, a courtesan.
- Bianca seems to have real feelings for Cassio, which are unrequited.
- He succeeds Othello as governor of Cyprus.

Roderigo is another potential suitor for Desdemona and, although he is cruelly used by Iago, there is something comic about him in the sense that he is a fool. He is taken in by Iago. In narrative terms, the audience are invited to see Iago at work duping Roderigo prior to his ensnarement of Othello, so part of his function is to introduce the reader to Iago's modus operandi, or way of doing things. You might see Roderigo as a contrast to Cassio in terms of their attributes as lovers and, although both suffer at the hands of the villainous ensign, Cassio advances, whereas Roderigo dies.

It is likely that most audiences feel little for Roderigo in spite of his treatment. This is possibly because of his foolishness in thinking he is able to win Desdemona's hand and also because of the way he allows himself to become involved in the plot against Othello. Iago describes him as a **'young quat'** *(Act 5, Scene 1)*. He appears weak and when he utters doubts about the way things are proceeding it takes very little effort on Iago's part to persuade him. Roderigo is not without moral merit though and, by the end of the tale, he realizes that his actions have made him a villain. He also understands, at the very moment of his death, that he has been used.

Brabantio

Like many other characters in the play, Brabantio, in his dual role as senator and duped father, is a victim of Iago's schemes. Before Act 1 is over, we have witnessed how Brabantio has very quickly been exploited to the point of fury. He serves a couple of important functions in the narrative, one of which is to help sow the seed of doubt about Desdemona – his ignorance of her marriage helps to show how a man's doubts about a woman can very quickly become feverous. This in turn prefigures Othello's experiences and so the audience gets an indication of how Iago's exploitation works its dark magic.

Shakespeare shows us that Brabantio appears to be balanced and well thought of. The Duke terms him 'gentle' *(Act 1, Scene 1)* and makes it clear that Brabantio's judgement is greatly valued. Othello himself reveals that Desdemona's father was fond of him. If you accept that Brabantio was, prior to Iago's intervention, a sympathetic, balanced character, then it becomes easier to see how jealousy, suspicion and manipulation can turn a good man bad. His love turns to anger, he refuses to allow Desdemona to lodge with him and he refuses to accept the version of events placed in front of him. These parallels with Othello's story act as an important structural device. Like the protagonist, Brabantio dies, heartbroken by his inability to see Desdemona for what she is.

Key quotations

       welcome, gentle signior;
We lack'd your counsel and your help tonight.
(Duke, Act 1, Scene 3)

But words are words; I never yet did hear
That the bruis'd heart was pierced through the ear.
(Brabantio, Act 1, Scene 3)

Poor Desdemon, I am glad thy father's dead:
Thy match was mortal to him, and pure grief
Shore his old thread in twain.
(Gratiano, Act 5, Scene 2)

Writing about characterization and roles

Thinking about characters in relation to their functions in the narrative will help you to see the way in which their stories contribute to the design of the play as a whole. Draw together the following elements and then conclude how the characters function within the play.

- Be alert for parallels between characters, especially the way in which the actions and words of one character are echoed by another.
- Look carefully at how characters appear to be archetypes, but also how the playwright gives them complexity, making them rounded rather than one-dimensional.
- Try to write about characters in relation to dramatic method. Explore, for example, who is given soliloquys and asides, and at which points in the narrative.
- Think about the character's journey in the story, and where they end up.
- Consider which characters gain the audience's sympathies and why. Which actions invite you to understand their suffering?
- Are you, as the audience, in possession of more information than the characters are?

Elevated language

Tragic plays, being interested in the darker aspects of the human condition, often treat their subject matter in a philosophical way, rendering excruciating experiences in an artistic manner. You will have noticed that tragic language can be lofty and artfully shaped; the protagonists, who are usually characters of status, offer their thoughts in elevated language, which means that the words rise above the ordinary, often in beautifully poetic ways.

Tragedy doesn't really attempt to capture ordinary or colloquial speech, and can seem artificial at times. It's highly unlikely, for instance, that in real life a person facing certain death would be able to utter a skilfully constructed speech that captures the essence of the human condition. But tragedies are art, not real life, so listening to the carefully crafted ways in which awful events are relayed is part of the joy of *Othello*.

> ### Activity 1
>
> Read Othello's speech from **'The tyrant custom…'** to **'I crave fit disposition of my wife'** in Act 1, Scene 3, where he accepts his role in Cyprus. Identify:
>
> - **figurative language**
> - imagery
> - complex **polysyllabic** words.

> **figurative language** figures of speech such as metaphor and **simile**
>
> **polysyllabic** consisting of several syllables
>
> **simile** a figure of speech comparing one thing with another, using 'like' or 'as'

As you will have noticed, the context of this speech within the play explains some of its formality. Othello is speaking to the Duke in the senate, so you might expect some high-register phrases. Yet you may find it a little strange that this man of action – Othello is a mercenary solider, after all – relates his answer to the Duke in such poetic ways. The personification of 'custom' as a tyrant, and the associations of toughness carried in words connected with strong materials, give Othello's tough-guy image an elevated quality. The respectful attitude and complex vocabulary all serve to reinforce the image of Othello in Act 1 as a controlled, thoughtful warrior-come-romantic lover.

One way Othello is characterized is through the range of references in his speech. The choice of language made by Shakespeare reveals a lot about the Moor's character. At times of emotion, the bombastic qualities in Othello's character emerge and the allusions to military matters give an insight into his values.

Activity 2

'Read Othello's speech from **'I had been happy…'** to **'Pride, pomp, and circumstance of glorious war!'** in Act 3, Scene 3, where he reflects on what he perceives to be his wife's infidelity. Explore:

- references to war
- the bombastic, exclamatory quality of the words
- repetition of words and grammatical structures.

This painting – *The Siege of Calais* by François-Édouard Picot – shows the 'pride, pomp, and circumstance' of 16th-century warfare

Key quotation

And, O you mortal engines, whose rude throats
Th'immortal Jove's dread clamours counterfeit,
Farewell! Othello's occupation's gone!
(Othello, Act 3, Scene 3)

Activity 3

Compare and contrast the two speeches you have looked at in Activities 1 and 2. What are the differences in the language and what explains them?

Linguistic patterns

Although writing about the rhythm of lines for its own sake is largely pointless, there may be times when you wish to link patterns of language to the possible meanings of the words or the ideas in the dialogue.

In the Genre chapter, you looked at Othello's thought patterns and justifications for his actions in the final scene of the play. The linguistic patterns repay investigation in his first speech in Act 5, Scene 2, from 'It is the cause...' to 'I'll smell it on the tree'. By this point, Othello is preparing to murder Desdemona and appears to have regained some composure.

The convention that the speech of important characters is written in **iambic pentameter** is followed here, with the rhythm of the lines suggesting a sense of control on the part of Othello. Consider the following extract:

It <u>is</u> the <u>cause</u>, it <u>is</u> the <u>cause</u>, my <u>soul</u>:
Let me not name it to you, you chaste stars.
It is the cause. Yet I'll not shed her blood,
Nor scar that whiter skin of hers than snow
(Othello, Act 5, Scene 2)

Here each line has ten syllables, which are grouped into five iambs. An **iamb** is two syllables comprising an unstressed and a stressed syllable. In the first line, the five stresses (or main beats) fall on 'is', 'cause', 'is', 'cause' and 'soul', as underlined. Although the line would never be delivered on stage in such a forced way, there is a pulse that resembles the general rhythm of English speech and is also conventional to some English poetry.

Activity 4

Identify the stresses in lines 2–4 of the extract above.

For the most part, Shakespeare is following the convention of the form, yet, in the example above, it is possible to see how the control Othello is trying to retain is reflected in the controlled, orderly speech patterns. Remember that at this point in the play he is preparing to kill a woman he loved and is wrestling with contradictory feelings. The justification he gives is an attempt to confer reason on his actions and it may well be that the orderly iambic pentameter gives the appearance of control too.

Another way to interpret the rhythm in this speech is to see it as Othello's attempt to unconvincingly hold things together. There's an oddity in his calmness at this point and you may view it as actually showing the utter desperation by which he attempts to convince himself he's right. Perhaps the orderly patterns ironically reveal his anguish as he tries to retain his composure at a time of emotional turmoil.

In a similar way, the repetition of lines and words in the speech as a whole may well betray his passion. The **euphemistic** choice of 'the cause' indicates Othello's inability to think about the nature of Desdemona's supposed crime, yet contrasts with the blunt use of **'Yet she must die'** further on in the same speech.

A range of references is employed, including imagery associated with light, nature and natural processes. The double meanings around **'put out the light'** (Othello is carrying a candle) and plucking the rose carry on the euphemistic references to death in Act 5, Scene 2. They also suggest that Othello continues to view his wife in a positive way, with both images carrying positive connotations.

The associations of 'white' with purity offer an interesting contrast to Othello's belief that his wife has been sullied. It appears that in spite of his decision to smother her, he still represents her in the way that he once thought of her.

There is also a field of references drawn from cosmology, mythology and religion, such as 'soul', 'stars', 'minister' and 'Promethean'. Taken together, it feels as if Othello now views himself as the hand of justice, performing an act that will prevent further disaster and delivering it in a rhythmically ordered manner, all of which suggests a control that may be simply a façade.

euphemistic using an indirect or vague expression in place of a blunt observation

iamb two syllables comprising an unstressed and a stressed syllable

iambic pentameter a rhythm, a line composed of five iambs

> **Key quotation**
>
> When I have pluck'd thy rose,
> I cannot give it vital growth again;
> (Othello, Act 5, Scene 2)

Activity 5

Consider what the word choice, images and patterns in Othello's first speech in Act 5, Scene 2, from **'It is the cause...'** to **'I'll smell it on the tree'**, suggest about him. Which of the following views seem most convincing to you? Explain your choice.

A	Othello is struggling with his emotions. His words suggest someone who wishes to remember the ideal image of Desdemona but also feels that she must pay for her supposed misdemeanour.
B	Othello's image of himself as avenger suggests his instability and megalomania. He sees himself as a messenger of the gods and may be touched by insanity.

Linguistic collapse

Othello's controlled, elevated speeches sometimes give way to more chaotic utterances. One of the ways Shakespeare relates Othello's emotional and mental turmoil at key moments is through disordered language, which contrasts with the orderly iambic pentameter seen elsewhere in the play. Perhaps the high point of this is in Acts 4 and 5, where Othello has allowed Iago's poison to work.

Iago's (Lucian Msamati) words poison Othello's (Hugh Quarshie) mind, Royal Shakespeare Company, 2015

Activity 6

Explore the linguistic patterns in the extracts below from Acts 4 and 5 and their effects. Consider:

- the brevity of utterances
- exclamations, questions and interjections
- repeated words and phrases.

A   From **'Lie with her? Lie on her?'** to **'Handkerchief? O devil!'** *(Othello, Act 4, Scene 1)*

B   From **'Yes – 'tis Emilia – by and by...'** to **'O insupportable! O heavy hour!'** *(Othello, Act 5, Scene 2)*

'Ordinary' language

Speech in fiction is never real, but playwrights can approximate real speech. Whether Shakespeare ever imitates real speech is debatable, but certainly in Iago's speech, we see less grandiose vocabulary and references. If Othello offers emotive, bombastic words at times, Iago's words seem more 'ordinary', perhaps reflecting his worldly, less grand intentions and his lesser status in the world of the play.

Iago's dialogue contains words that focus on tangible, less intellectual ideas than Othello's. Othello's poetic references to Hellespont and **'Promethean heat'**, for example, alongside his tales of daring, contrast with Iago's more commonplace concerns about purses, strumpets and asses. To say Iago's language is base and demotic is too simplistic. His flexibility with situations sees him alter, chameleon-like, from the direct, imperative character who instructs Roderigo in Act 4, Scene 2 to the slippery, apparently servile man who manipulates Othello.

Activity 7

Carefully study the three extracts from Iago's dialogue below. Compare:

- the nature of the nouns – whether they are **concrete** or **abstract**
- the register and complexity of the words
- the philosophical or prosaic qualities of his speech
- who he is addressing
- whether the speech is in prose or verse.

A From 'I never found a man...' to 'I would change my humanity with a baboon' *(Act 1, Scene 3)*

B From 'Good my lord, pardon me...' to 'Why, say they are vile and false?' *(Act 3, Scene 3)*

C From 'I have rubb'd this young quat...' to 'As gifts to Desdemona' *(Act 5, Scene 1)*

---

abstract noun an idea, quality or state; something that does not exist as a material object

concrete noun a thing you can experience through the use of your five senses (touch, taste, smell, sight, hearing)

Persuasive language

Iago's manipulation is built on words. His skill at persuasive oratory may be admired, even if his intentions are bad. The central scene – Act 3, Scene 3 – offers the audience a masterclass in the dark arts of linguistic manipulation. Iago is shown to have improvisational qualities, responding to situations in what seems like a flexible way. He also schemes and very carefully lays the traps for Othello.

In Act 3, Scene 3, you will notice that Iago employs a range of strategies:

- **Implication and withholding** In the lines from 'My noble lord –' to 'No further harm', Iago attracts Othello's attention in a way that invites the Moor to wonder if Iago has something significant to say. Iago introduces the provocative topic of Cassio and Desdemona, and then, once he has Othello's attention, attempts to close down the conversation. The effect is to make Othello think that Iago possesses some key knowledge.

- **Denial of a fact** In the lines from 'Cassio, my lord?' to 'Seeing you coming', Iago pretends that he hasn't seen Cassio, even when it's clear to Othello that he has. Coupled with Iago's emphasis on guilt and secrecy, Othello's suspicions are raised.

- **Feigning loyalty and advising** In the lines from 'I am glad of this...' to 'Look to your wife, observe her well with Cassio', Iago puts himself in the position of sycophant. This servility appears to convince Othello, who believes that Iago has his best interests at heart, at which point Iago instructs Othello to be wary of Cassio. The advice chimes with Othello's fear.

- **Taking the opposite line** In the lines from 'My friend is dead...' to 'I am your own for ever', Iago plays devil's advocate, suggesting a view that provokes Othello into adopting the opposite perspective. Iago suggests that Desdemona deserves to live, prompting Othello to pronounce her death.

Activity 8

Consider Iago's tactics in extracts A–E below, all from Act 3, Scene 3. Which of the strategies listed above are used by Iago in the extracts below? Are there any different strategies being used by Iago?

A From 'Why then, I think Cassio's an honest man...' to 'The worst of words'

B She did deceive her father, marrying you; And when she seem'd to shake and fear your looks / She lov'd them most

C My lord, I would I might entreat your honour / To scan this thing no farther.

D And may. But how? How satisfied, my lord? / Would you, the supervisor, grossly gape on? / Behold her topp'd?

E From 'Nay, yet be wise...' to 'Spotted with strawberries in your wife's hand?'

Symbolism

A motif is an object that appears several times in a narrative but has meaningful qualities beyond being a mere object. Very often, a motif takes on different meanings as it reappears in the story. The handkerchief may be read as a motif in *Othello*. It has symbolic qualities and seems to mean different things to different characters at different times.

The handkerchief is circulated between the characters and also features as part of the backstory of Othello's history. It has a narrative significance in that the plot is driven in part by Iago's appropriation of it. It is passed from character to character and, as it is, reveals a lot about the themes of the play. The handkerchief was woven in silk by a female prophet (a sibyl) and then it is passed to Othello's father or mother (Othello gives differing accounts). Othello gives it to Desdemona, who loses it. It is then found by Emilia, taken by Iago, planted in Cassio's chamber, and then given to Bianca. Each character views the value and significance of this square of ornamental material in different ways.

Linking the handkerchief to the preserved bodies of virgins, nature and the sacred suggests a strong thematic link to issues of female chastity and primitive beliefs. Othello appears to abandon his logic and retreat into superstition.

Activity 9

Consider the account of the origin of the handkerchief given by Othello in Act 3, Scene 4, from **'There's magic in the web of it…'** to **'Conserv'd of maidens' hearts'**.

a) What does it reveal about Othello's beliefs?

b) How does this contrast with the measured, logical Othello we see in Act 1?

Activity 10

Explore Othello's speech in Act 3, Scene 4, from **'That's a fault…'** to **'As nothing else could match'**, in which he tells Desdemona about the handkerchief.

a) What new light does it shed on the way Othello views love and fidelity?

b) How do you interpret Desdemona's minimal response? Bear in mind that by this point, Desdemona has misplaced the item and is reluctant to tell Othello.

To Othello, the handkerchief symbolizes his love for Desdemona. It is a literal love token, but also represents his feelings and commitment. It has sentimental value too, given its link to Othello's mother. The loss of the hand-kerchief equates (in Othello's mind) to the loss of his wife. Desdemona also sees the handkerchief as a valuable, symbolic item. To Iago, it is merely a means of ensnaring Othello.

Although a symbol of innocence, the handkerchief is crucial to Iago's (Antony Sher) evil plot, Royal Shakespeare Company, 2007

Imagery

Literary texts make use of images to illuminate themes and central ideas. In *Othello*, a range of images is drawn from nature, colour and the human body. Some images take literal qualities, such as blackness, and use them in a metaphorical way. Many ideas in the play work around opposite concepts, such as light and dark. The language itself, and the way in which it is corrupted and misconstrued, expresses the themes that tie the play together.

Oppositional imagery

One of the central ideas of the play is that of 'turning Turk'; Othello used the phrase **'turn'd Turks'** to mean metaphorically switching sides *(Act 2, Scene 3)*. In the play, there are several instances of characters moving from certainty to doubt, love to hate, friend to enemy, and honour to dishonour. The imagery in the play is, in part, based on oppositions; one of which is related to the skin colour of the characters.

On stage, Othello's otherness – his race and outsider status – is quite literally shown in the colour of his face. The associations of race were explored earlier in the Context chapter, but it is now worth exploring what is signified by the adjectives 'black' and 'white' in the world of the play. The original audience would have been familiar with the negative associations of black that persisted in contemporary literature and society. Today, the pejorative connotations of words such as 'blackball', 'black magic', 'blacklist' and 'black humour' suggest that language still reflects assumptions about colour that continue to reinforce negative views. By contrast, white and its associations with purity, innocence and light enjoys a much more positive frame of reference.

Activity 11

Discuss with a partner the concept of 'blackening' somebody, specifically the process by which Iago blackens Desdemona's name. Is it actually the case that white characters perpetrate the most evil in the play? Or is this view too simplistic?

Nature imagery

Images connected with nature are often assumed to be positive: humans have a tendency to ascribe sentimental, pastoral qualities to nature. Images of Mother Nature as fertile and bountiful are familiar ones, and in some texts, nature is presented as truthful, wise and ungoverned by man's corruption.

Activity 12

Explore the way images of black and white are used in the extracts below. Consider:

- who is speaking and what is happening at that point in the play
- how references to colour are being used
- whether it is possible to say that black and white are always used to signify good and bad .

A **Even now, now, very now, an old black ram / Is tupping your white ewe.** *(lago, Act 1, Scene 1)*

B From **'Whether a maid so tender, fair, and happy...'** to **'... to fear, not to delight'** *(Brabantio, Act 1, Scene 2)*

C **And noble signior, / If virtue no delighted beauty lack, / Your son-in-law is far more fair than black.** *(Duke, Act 1, Scene 3)*

D **Her name, that was as fresh / As Dian's visage, is now begrim'd and black / As mine own face.** *(Othello, Act 3, Scene 3)*

E From **'Arise, black vengeance, from thy hollow cell...'** to **'For 'tis of aspics' tongues'** *(Othello, Act 3, Scene 3)*

F **Nor I neither by this heavenly light; / I might do't as well I'th'dark.** *(Emilia, Act 4, Scene 3)*

G From **'Let me now name it to you...'** to **'And smooth as monumental alabaster'** *(Othello, Act 5, Scene 2)*

H **O, the more angel she, / And you the blacker devil!** *(Emilia, Act 5, Scene 2)*

However, you only need consider the symbolism of the snake in the Garden of Eden to see that how we read natural imagery depends very much upon the context in which it is used. In Iago's speech, from **'Virtue? A fig!'** *(Act 1, Scene 3)*, Shakespeare employs several horticultural metaphors. Here Iago's words contain the argument that however we choose to act is entirely our own business – he tells Roderigo that anything is in your power and that, like gardeners deciding which plants to grow, it is one's desires and drive that determine success.

Activity 13

Iago uses many references to the animal world. Locate the following animals in the text and consider the connotations of these animals in the context of the dialogue.

- Ass
- Beast
- Jennets

- Snipe
- Baboon
- Coursers

- Monkey
- Toad
- Barbary horse

- Goat
- Ram

Activity 14

Below is a list of three types of imagery in the play. Locate as many references in the play linked to these images as you can, perhaps using an online text locator.

a) Vision References to sight and seeing abound in the play, with an obvious double meaning around the concepts of perception and not seeing/misunderstanding. Othello's desire for **'ocular proof'** *(Act 3, Scene 3)* is central to his undoing.

b) Blood There are violent episodes in the text that lead to bloodshed, but blood can also have a metaphorical dimension, signifying passion and loss of virginity.

c) Water The literal crossing of the sea features in Act 2 and there are many references to the physical aspect of water, including Othello having several lines of dialogue based around sea images.

Double meanings

Concepts such as 'seeing' have obvious double meanings relating to sight and perception. In a play in which the villain manipulates language, it is no surprise that some regularly used words in the play take on double meanings. In some cases, the ambiguity around word meanings causes fatal misunderstanding between characters.

The words 'lie' and 'lying' occur more than 20 times in the text and a great deal is made of the multiple meanings, which on one hand mean to tell an untruth and on the other mean to occupy a bed. The pun is made explicit in the lines from **'Do you know, sirrah, where Lieutenant Cassio lies?'** to **'... were to lie in mine own throat'** *(Act 3, Scene 4)*, when Desdemona has her conversation with the Clown.

There is a cruel irony that Iago tells a lie that suggests that Cassio and Desdemona have been lying together. The horrible image it conjures up in the lines **'Lie –'** to **'Lie with her!'** causes Othello to fall into a trance in Act 4, Scene 1.

The linguistic concept of double meanings also finds its expression in the plot and characters of the play. Othello's dual explanation of the handkerchief's origins, and the dual terms afforded to Iago – who is both 'honest' and a 'knave', alongside Desdemona's supposed deceit of her father and husband, help to reinforce the play's exploration of ambiguity and deceit.

Repetition

As well as structural repetition in the plot, such as Desdemona's supposed deception, certain words are reiterated in the text. The word 'bed' makes its appearance 20 times and 'honest' occurs more than 50 times. Given the play's concentration on sex, truth and deception, this is no surprise.

Yet 'honest' is often used in dramatically ironic terms. Iago, the most dishonest character in the play, is referred to as **'Honest Iago'** by Othello in Act 1, Scene 3. By this point, the audience is aware of Iago's desire to punish Othello and so the term itself comes to mean the reverse when applied to the Ensign.

Activity 15

Find all the uses of 'honest' in the text. How many times is it used in its original meaning and how often is it used in a way that suggests the reverse?

Writing about language

When you write about language, never do it in isolation. You will not say much by simply spotting features. Instead, points about language should be linked closely to ideas about meaning and character. This chapter has focused on the larger features of language such as imagery and patterns, and what they reveal about the ideas in the play. There may be times when exploring the connotations of single words is useful because it illuminates an aspect of character.

Performance

The decisions made by a director and actors can strongly influence the way a character or scene is received by the audience. If you read a novel, the action takes place in your head, but a drama script takes place on stage and there is a group of people – the director and actors – creating an interpretation of the play, one which may or may not coincide with the version you have in your head.

Unlike playwrights such as Arthur Miller or Tennessee Williams, Shakespeare's stage directions are minimal, and so there is plenty of scope for how scenes may be performed and how lines may be delivered. As you study the play, be alert to the ways in which performance context can affect the way the play is interpreted. As ever, there is no 'correct' reading of the play, so exploring the performance history of the play over time, and thinking about the subtle differences of many productions, will illuminate your study of the text.

Performance as a reading

Period setting, costume, gesture, body language and delivery all contribute to performance and, in deciding such things, a reading of a text is produced. Different directors will often have an overall vision of the play, which will be affected by their personal context. One way to explore the importance of performance context is to consider what sort of decisions you might make about delivery.

Activity 1

Read the lines from **'Who's there? Othello?'** to **'Hum!'** *(Act 5, Scene 2)*, which come after Othello, as he prepares to kill Desdemona, has delivered his **'smooth as monumental alabaster'** speech at the beginning of the same scene and Desdemona has woken up. As you read, consider how you imagine the lines being performed on stage.

Othello prepares to kill Desdemona.

Here are several considerations about the performance of the lines from **'Who's there? Othello?'** to **'Hum!'** *(Act 5, Scene 2)*, which might influence the way you view the characters and their situation.

- How is Desdemona's first line delivered? She has just woken up. Does she see Othello appearing distracted and deliver the line tremulously, as if she knows something is wrong? Or does she smile lovingly as she squints in the darkness and recognizes her husband?

- Where precisely is Othello standing as he addresses his wife? Is he close to the bed, looking intently at the woman he is about to smother, or is he further away with his back turned, ashamed to think of his crime?

- Does Desdemona realize the importance of Othello's enquiry, **'Have you pray'd'**? Is there a gap between the question and her response? If there is a pause, what might it signify? Her confusion or her growing suspicion of his conduct?

- How does Desdemona react when Othello utters the word **'kill'**? Is she aghast? Or does her face convey a real sense of naivety and a genuine inability to comprehend? How does Othello utter the word 'kill'? Quietly, as if he can't bear to think about it? Or in monotone, which might suggest a more sinister approach to the deed?

- Is Othello's line **'Amen, with all my heart!'** delivered with extreme passion? Is 'heart' emphasized to express his love for her?

- How is **'Hum!'** delivered? Dismissively? What does Desdemona's face convey at this point?

Activity 2

Consider each of the points above. How do you see each line in the extract working in performance? What overall effect do you feel needs to be achieved in this extract?

Activity 3

Continuing to think about the lines from **'Who's there? Othello?'** to **'Hum!'** *(Act 5, Scene 2)*, consider the following two descriptions of possible performances of the scene and what is shown about each character. Which, if any, coincides with your view of this extract?

Performance A

From the moment Desdemona awakes, the scene is one of dread for both characters. In the dim light she realizes from her husband's distant manner and taut body language that her life is under threat. He is standing some distance from her bed, barely making eye contact. Her voice, wavering, tries to distract her husband by inviting him to bed. Othello isn't interested, however. His manner is cold, as if he is shutting out emotion. Although he dreads what is to come, he has managed to bury any feelings. His lines are delivered in a level manner, until he dismisses his wife's fear with a belittling 'Hum!'

Performance B

A naive Desdemona wakes to find her husband sat on the edge of her bed. She assumes that he has come to make peace and she wants him to come to bed. His voice is shaky. It has taken quite some time to face what he is about to do and he still has grave doubts in spite of his earlier decision. For a moment he pauses, considering whether to join her in bed. But then his emotional engagement ceases and his speech takes on a more commanding air. He is set on his purpose and, as the temperature of the scene rises, his words are delivered loudly. Desdemona's fear sets in when she finally realizes that he intends to kill her. As she pleads with him, she reaches out, clutching his sleeve. He snatches it away and looks blankly into her eyes as he sarcastically spits out 'Amen, with all my heart!'

Activity 4

Choose your own extract from the play and think about the different ways it might be performed. Write two differing versions describing the extract, using the models in Activity 2 as templates.

Concepts underpinning performance

Most directors begin with an overall concept, idea or plan of the play and use this to inform key decisions about staging, costume and movement. Some productions are set in what might be considered a traditional way, adopting versions of 17th-century costume and using staging that suggests the Venice and Cyprus of the time. Other directors select modern dress and place the text in a more modern world, which can help an audience to see the play through fresh eyes or perhaps make the point that the play's ideas are universal to any time.

Activity 5

Nicholas Hytner, in his Royal Shakespeare Company (RSC) production of the play, set the play in the British Army at an unspecified point in the previous 25 years. Read *The Telegraph* review on the next page and consider:

a) What was added by setting the play in recognizable locations?

b) How foregrounding the military aspect might help an audience to understand Othello and Iago's relationship.

The director passionately believes that Shakespeare is our contemporary, and the action moves from a recognisable modern London of pubs, blaring pop music and an emergency Cabinet meeting to a British military base in Cyprus, a grim redoubt of reinforced concrete, orange sodium streetlights and cheerless accommodation. [...]

The scenes in which Iago winds up Othello to a jealousy that trips over into epileptic fits and mental derangement are hideously compelling. Kinnear appears to be improvising his evil on the hoof, with the most memorable encounter taking place in the army camp lavatories where Othello spews up in a cubicle as his faith in his wife collapses. It is an appropriate choice of location for Iago, a man only really at home in a moral sewer.

(Charles Spencer, *The Telegraph*, 24 April 2013)

Activity 6

Iqbal Khan's RSC production also emphasized the military background, but made an interesting choice in casting a black actor to play Iago. It also went some way to undermining the idea of Othello as a noble character, implying that the use of military torture was not unfamiliar to him.

Read the review from *The Guardian* below and consider what is added by casting a black actor in the villain's role and whether you think the choice to reveal a less savoury side to Othello fits with your reading of the play.

For a start, it reinforces the historic bond between Othello and Iago, and helps to explain the trust the former places in his ensign. By making Othello the commander of a multi-racial unit, Khan also exposes the unresolved tensions in the group: you can see exactly why Iago would detest a Caucasian Cassio who tries to show his kinship with the men by taking part in a rap contest during the Cypriot drinking scene. And one of Khan's shrewdest touches, in this modern-dress production, is to dismantle the stereotype of Othello as the 'noble Moor' by showing that he sanctions waterboarding by his troops and is prepared to use torture to get Iago to cough up details of Desdemona's presumed infidelity.

(Michael Billington, *The Guardian*, 12 June 2015)

Representing race

One of the controversies that has dogged the play is the choice of actor playing Othello and whether it is desirable to cast a white man in the role. Although the text makes it clear that Othello is a man of colour, most historical Othellos have been played by white actors, quite probably because of the scarcity of black actors in earlier centuries. In recent times, the role has become the preserve of black actors. The first major production starring a black actor, Ira Aldridge, was in the 1830s. In 1930, Paul Robeson starred in the title role, causing some disquiet for audiences at the spectacle of a black man physically controlling a white woman, thus revealing a great deal about the cultural ideas of the time in 1930s America.

Sensitivity around race has led to many critical debates around whether the role can ever justifiably be played by a white actor. Michael Gambon, in 1990, was probably the last white actor to play the role wearing black make-up. The issue of skin colour has its origins in Lawrence Olivier's performance of the role in black-face at the National Theatre in the 1960s. Although incredibly well received, the concept is now viewed with displeasure in some circles, as this review explains:

> […] it is offensive to black people to see a white actor put on dark make-up and pretend to be black. Not only is it politically and culturally offensive, with hazy memories of *The Black and White Minstrel Show* with its Uncle Tom gestures; it is also offensive because Equity has a disproportionate number of unemployed black actors on its books. How galling it would be for them, let alone the black community as a whole, to see a white actor transform himself into a black man.
>
> (www.independent.co.uk – David Lister, 6 August 1997)

Activity 7

How far do you agree that a white actor playing Othello is problematic? Start by considering the following statements:

A	'Great drama is colour-blind and goes far deeper than the colour of a person's skin, white or black' (Steven Berkoff, quoted by Jess Denham, *The Independent*, 16 June 2015)

B	'The theatre is not real life. It is a place for artifice, which depends on disguise and dressing up. The disguising of a white actor for the role of the Moor is a 400-year-old tradition. Tradition does not justify something that is morally wrong. But is it really morally wrong to do this in the sphere of acting, where pretence is of the essence?' (www.independent.co.uk – David Lister, 6 August 1997)

Activity 8

Patrick Stewart portrayed Othello in 1997 in an unorthodox version of the play, where the white veteran British actor played Othello surrounded by an African-American cast, in what its director called 'the photo negative Othello'.

a) How might this choice of casting affect the way in which the ideas of the play might be received by various audiences?

b) How might the sight of a white Othello surrounded by an otherwise black cast affect the way you interpret the play?

Patrick Stewart plays Othello with an otherwise all-black cast, including Patrice Johnson as Desdemona, Shakespeare Theatre Company, Washington DC, 1997 (Photo by Carol Rosegg)

Performing Othello

The role of Othello is demanding for an actor, requiring the controlled nobility of the earlier scenes and the physicality of his descent into passionate madness. It is generally noted that there are two 'types' of Othello: one that emphasizes the dignity and poeticism of the character and one that gives more weight to his passion and dangerous energy.

The first Othello, Richard Burbage, was a leading actor of the period and performed the role in 1604. Here are some other notable representations of the role:

● **Ira Aldridge, 1826** Aldridge was the first African-American Othello, appearing at London's Royalty Theatre. Some critics of the time objected to the sight of a black man manhandling a white woman.

- **Samuel Phelps and William Macready, 1837** Innovatively, these actors played both Othello and Iago, switching between roles on alternate nights, an approach also adopted by Richard Burton and John Neville in the 1950s.

- **Tommaso Salvini, 1869** An Italian actor who performed the play in his native language, Salvini was renowned for his incredible intensity. Desdemona's murder was particularly aggressively played, to the point where it is believed that some actors lined up to play his wife were reluctant to appear.

- **Paul Robeson, 1930** A renowned singer, athlete, lawyer and offspring of a former slave, Robeson's portrayal of Othello at the Savoy Theatre was a phenomenal success. In the 1940s, perhaps more significantly, Robeson played the role on Broadway, where for the first time an American audience witnessed a black man kiss a white woman on stage.

- **Susanne Wolff, 2011** In this production, Othello was rendered as a white woman in love with a female Desdemona. There was a lot of focus on costume, with Othello appearing in everyday clothing before donning a gorilla suit on learning of her wife's supposed infidelity.

Activity 9

It is often said that performances of *Othello* tell us a great deal about the culture we live in. How far do you think this view is reflected in the various performances described above and in film versions you have seen?

Performing Iago

In the wrong hands, Iago could become little more than a pantomime villain. It is possible to imagine a cruelly comedic Iago who delights the audience with his sinuous manipulation and joyous sense of *schadenfreude*, taking pleasure at his boss's downfall. The challenge for an actor playing the part is to find a way between Iago's obvious power and his damaged powerlessness.

Iago appears in most of the scenes. He is on stage more than Othello and, in some ways, is a more interesting character than the Moor. It is possible to imagine a version of the text entitled 'Iago', which centralizes the Ensign and his actions. The fact that a villain is given so many soliloquies invites us to try to understand the character, rather than simply condemn him. Perhaps there is a tragedy in his story.

When asked whose play it was – Othello's or Iago's – Rory Kinnear (then playing Iago) suggested equal billing, observing:

> In the first half Iago is the engine of the play, but it gets to a point where he's no longer the puppeteer. He's just trying desperately to keep all the plates spinning, and it becomes very much this appalling tragedy of a man in absolute torment. But Shakespeare's great trick […] is to make the audience complicit in Iago's villainy. He's afforded seven soliloquies to get them onside. That's part of the horrendous joy of the play.
>
> (www.theguardian.co.uk – Stephen Moss, 10 April 2013)

Finding a way to play Iago, which exposes his cruelty but also his superficial care, is part of the challenge. Some actors express the view that Shakespeare's text does not really offer a consistent view of Iago that allows a director or actor to decide how to play the villain. British actor Ian McKellen explained how he decided to approach the role:

> Within his confessional asides, Iago makes his motives clear. I wouldn't have known how to play the critical cliché of the man as the embodiment of all evil. So I played the jealous husband who suspects 'the lustful Moor hath leaped into my seat' and can urge his boss to 'beware of jealousy' because he himself is a victim of it. This, plus what he takes to be Cassio's unfair promotion over him, is more than enough for him to hate.
>
> (Ian McKellen, www.mckellen.com, May 2003)

Activity 10

Experiment with the different ways that Iago's speech, from **'I lay with Cassio…'** to **'to the Moor'** *(Act 3, Scene 3)*, might be delivered. In it, Iago is fictionalizing a dream in which he claims to have heard Cassio incriminate himself. Consider:

- which words and lines should be given emphasis
- where dramatic pauses may be placed
- the overall image of Iago. Is he delivering these lines in an overacted manner? Is he understated, almost apologetic?

Performing Desdemona

Actors playing Desdemona can run the risk of being overshadowed by Iago and Othello, becoming little more than the naive victim. Desdemona offers scope for interpretation though, and one of the central decisions for any production is whether she has a sense of agency in the world of the play or whether she is utterly passive.

A range of Desdemonas have been offered during the production history of the play. One way of seeing her is as a daughter who is always viewed through her father's words. It is also possible to go against this reading and offer a performance that suggests a much more empowered, witty and sexually mature character, who in the end falls victim to the world of men. Consider the following review of the play and the version of Desdemona produced:

 There was nothing passive about Olivia Vinall's Desdemona. She brought to the role a fully-realized sexuality and a femininity, which was attractive because it wasn't trying to satisfy the obvious patriarchal demands of the very male-dominated world she has to inhabit. It made her vibrantly present to the desires of Roderigo and allowed her to reflect the casual flirtations of Cassio.

(www.bloggingshakespeare.com – 2013)

Olivia Vinall's Desdemona provides a counter-balance to Adrian Lester's Othello, Royal National Theatre, 2013

Activity 11

Key scenes in the play require thought as to how Desdemona is played. Consider the issues thrown up by the following parts of the play:

a) From 'Where most you owe obedience?' to 'Due to the Moor my lord' *(Act 1, Scene 3)* and from 'That I did love the Moor to live with him...' to 'Let me go with him' *(Act 1, Scene 3)*. These are the audience's first glimpses of Desdemona, where she diplomatically defends her husband and states her case to depart with him to Cyprus. The text appears to suggest a woman who is at ease speaking in a public forum. But is this conveyed in the manner of delivery? Should the audience get a sense of her need to pacify, if not please, the various men in her life? How does Othello react to his wife's speeches? How does her father react? Is she viewed as active and decisive by the Duke or as a pleading, powerless young wife?

b) From 'The riches of the ship is come on shore!' to 'What tidings can you tell me of my lord?' *(Act 2, Scene 1)* and from 'Be thou assur'd, good Cassio...' to 'Than give thy cause away' *(Act 3, Scene 3)*. When she talks with Cassio, how does she act? Does she respond to the flattery he offers? Is she playful and coquettish? Does the audience need to see a Desdemona who is completely devoted to Othello or should they glimpse a slightly flirtatious, sexually aware woman who enjoys Cassio's words and courtly manner?

c) **Act 5, Scene 2** Desdemona's death scene offers plenty of room for interesting versions of the character. Does she willingly submit? Does she struggle? How does she deliver her final lines, when she appears to accept the blame herself?

Writing about performance

In your writing, you will need to use performance context carefully. There is no advantage in listing features of various productions you may have seen unless they are directly relevant to the question that faces you. Writing about performance works best when linked to the overarching concepts and ideas in the play.

If you are exploring an extract from *Othello* closely, you may well choose to focus on a specific key line from the text and write about various ways the performance of the line might give rise to different readings of character.

Be careful not to confuse the study of literature with theatre studies – the primary focus is the text and its meanings. Dramatic method and performance aspects should only support the points you make about the literary aspects of the play.

Themes

Themes help to unify a story. They often explore moral ideas – concepts that seem applicable to the lives of most people. Themes such as jealousy and deception are prevalent in *Othello* and are explored through the actions of different characters and scenes. These themes invite us to see the text as having a kind of unity of design – an ordered, shaped message that comes to represent what is 'meant' by *Othello*. In seeing thematic ideas played and replayed during the course of the play, members of the audience come to see what they consider to be 'the point' of the story. As with character and performance, however, themes can be interpreted in various ways and can provoke a range of readings.

Activity 1

By this point in your studies, you should be able to identify the main ideas arising from the play. Write a list of the overarching concepts and recurring ideas that you see as central to the story of *Othello*.

Jealousy

Perhaps the main theme of the play is that of sexual jealousy, which is often an unwanted by-product of love. Jealousy can be viewed as an indicator of insecurity and obsession. Jealousy in Shakespeare's time was generally seen as an extension of the sin of envy and regarded as a destructive force, often leading to violent confrontation, sometimes death. The play explores the destructive effects of jealousy, tracing how Othello moves from a noble, loving husband to a man whose mistrust of his wife is such that he kills her.

The recognizable human emotion of sexual jealousy is explored in the main body of the play, but jealousy is introduced in the first lines of the play, when Iago expresses a different type – professional jealousy – about Cassio's promotion. Cassio has been made lieutenant and therefore enjoys a higher status than Iago. If we take Iago at his word (the reliability of which is a matter for debate), then it seems that his own jealousy spurs him on to act against Othello. One view of the play might be that we see how jealousy can be a motivating force for revenge and that one person's jealousy leads in turn to another's, until the matter is resolved by death.

Activity 2

What is the nature of Iago's complaint about Cassio as related in Act 1 Scene 1, from **'One Michael Cassio…'** to **'Is all his soldiership'**? Consider:

- Cassio's personal qualities
- Cassio's leadership and soldierly qualities.

84

Activity 3

Iago's motives are, it seems, governed by jealousy. Read the extracts listed below and consider:

- how Iago feels towards Desdemona
- what Iago suspects Othello of and the effect it has upon him
- how Iago views the effects of his own jealousy
- Iago's advice to Othello about jealousy and the extent to which he is speaking of his own predicament.

A 'Now, I do love here too, / Not out of absolute lust –'*(Iago, Act 2, Scene 1)*

B 'For that I do suspect the lusty Moor / Hath leap'd into my seat, the thought whereof / Doth like a poisonous mineral gnaw my inwards' *(Iago, Act 2, Scene 1)*

C 'As I confess it is my natures' plague / To spy into abuses, and oft my jealousy / Shapes faults that are not' *(Iago, Act 3, Scene 3)*

D 'Oh beware, my lord, of jealousy: / It is the green-eyed monster which doth mock / The meat it feeds on.' *(Iago, Act 3, Scene 3)*

Othello's jealousy is provoked through insinuation and the seeming **'ocular proof'** of the handkerchief *(Act 3, Scene 3)*. Iago's subtle words suggest that Cassio steals away **'guilty-like'** and, when Othello misunderstands her use of the term **'suitor'** in regard to Cassio, the suspicion of sexual misconduct has an incredibly destructive effect. The seed of jealousy, once planted, grows in Othello and is liberally watered by Iago.

Othello struggles to shake off his fears, but the wiser part of him proclaims that some sort of proof is essential. Perhaps his initial error is to allow Iago's suggestions to make him wish for proof, rather than simply trusting Desdemona. Othello's world collapses and he likens his despair to the chaos that existed before the Creation of Earth.

Key quotations

> when I love thee not
> Chaos is come again.   *(Othello, Act 3, Scene 3)*

> Nor from mine own weak merits will I draw
> The smallest fear or doubt of her revolt,
> For she had eyes and chose me. No, Iago,
> I'll see before I doubt   *(Othello, Act 3, Scene 3)*

Activity 4

Consider the following statements about jealousy in the play. Find evidence and examples from the text to support or challenge them.

A	The play traces the destructive effects of jealousy. It shows that humans are weak creatures who allow themselves to give in to their basic mistrust of others. The play confirms that even the most noble are susceptible to fear.

B	The play confirms that male pride and the need to control women is at the heart of the tragedy. Everything could have been avoided if Othello simply refused to give credit to Iago's insinuations. Fear of cuckoldry drives the events of the play.

C	All of the main characters in the text are jealous of somebody else, for reasons of sexual, familial or professional jealousy. The play paints a very poor picture of human conduct.

D	Most of the jealousies in the play are founded on little, so as well as appearing to be a highly destructive emotion, there is something ridiculous about the effects it has upon the characters, making humans seem a pathetic race.

Disorder and chaos

Tragic plays are concerned in part with disorder – the audience is shown societies and domestic arrangements being torn apart. Tragedy explores how fate, time and human weakness bring about disharmony before usually restoring a sense of balance, often through the deaths of the central characters. Disorder in *Othello* is therefore a structural aspect, in that we see the movement from Othello's nobility in the early scenes to his tumult. Only his death seems to bring an end to the chaos that emerges in Act 3.

Disorder is also a thematic aspect to the play, and several scenes present the audience with action where disruption and antagonism are central. Most tragedies commence with scenes of order, establishing the status quo that is about to be challenged. *Othello*, however, begins in the street and we see Iago and Roderigo break the peace of the Venetian streets when they shout for Brabantio.

Activity 5

Read the lines from **'Call up her father…'** to **'Is spied in populous cities'** *(Iago, Act 1, Scene 1)*. What images are used to symbolize the disorder that the antagonists bring upon Brabantio? What is their significance?

Othello himself acknowledges that when his love for his wife is brought into question, then **'chaos is come again'** *(Act 3, Scene 3)*. Othello's marriage to Desdemona may be seen, in itself, as a disorderly event by some of the citizens of Venice, giving rise to fears of miscegenation. Brabantio certainly sees his daughter's conduct as disorderly, as she has not observed the customary rules of her society. In neglecting to seek her father's permission to marry, and choosing an unconventional partner, Desdemona's actions create conflict.

The values of Venice and its senate act as a force of order in the play, with the Duke conferring a calm judgement upon matters. When the action moves to Cyprus, unruly passions and events occur, suggesting the island's outpost status is mirrored in its distance from convention. During the course of the play disorder takes many forms, sometimes physical, sometimes emotional.

The National Theatre production in 2013 portrayed Shakespeare's 'Cyprus' as a military outpost in an unspecified location, with Adrian Lester as Othello and Rory Kinnear as Iago

Activity 6

Read the extracts below. What effects, if any, do these disorderly events have in the remainder of the play? How is order restored?

A From **'The Ottomites...'** to **'... with an after fleet'** *(Messenger, Act 1, Scene 3)*

B From **'What from the cape...'** to **'Descry a sail'** *(Montano and First Gentleman, Act 2, Scene 1)*

C From **'Do not think, gentlemen...'** to **'... and I speak well enough'** *(Cassio, Act 2, Scene 3)*

D From **'Who's that which rings the bell?'** to **'Hold for your lives!'** *(Act 2, Scene 3)*

Appearance and reality

In a play about deceit, the theme of appearance and reality is central. Othello appears on the surface to be noble and balanced, yet turns out to be at the mercy of his emotions and, whatever the justification, he is a murderer. Iago appears (to the characters rather than the audience) to be 'honest', yet is anything but. Desdemona, in Othello's eyes, appears to be a 'strumpet', but in reality, is pure and innocent. After Othello realizes his error, he draws attention to his wife's appearance, which is both literally and symbolically white.

> **Key quotation**
>
> **Now, how dost thou look now? O ill-starr'd wench!**
> **Pale as thy smock!**
> *(Othello, Act 5, Scene 2)*

The 'alabaster' Desdemona remains pure, despite Iago's dishonouring of her. The play features several instances of 'seeing', but quite often Othello is won over by the false version of Desdemona portrayed by Iago. Even when Othello looks carefully at his wife's outward appearance at the start of Act 4, Scene 2, he refuses to associate her fairness with virtue and, in fact, sees her appearance as a deception.

> **Activity 7**
>
> Explore the words used in Othello's speech to Desdemona in Act 4, Scene 2, from **'Turn thy complexion there...'** to **'... would thou hadst ne'er been born!'.** Consider the images given of nature and corruption. How do they link to the theme of appearance and reality?

The theme of appearance and reality also finds its expression in the colour terms employed both literally and symbolically in the text. The dramatic spectacle of Othello's black face in a cast of white actors immediately draws attention to issues of race and otherness. As noted above, Desdemona is often described by her husband in terms connected with whiteness.

To the audience, this works symbolically, emphasizing her purity and innocence. She is a **'pearl'** and in life and death is associated with virtue. But the associations of **'black'** become ever more problematic in the play.

Iago, Roderigo and Brabantio's disparaging use of racial language foregrounds the issue in early scenes. Desdemona's defence of Othello in Act 1, Scene 3 links Othello's external appearance with the qualities of his persona when she tells the senate that **'I saw Othello's visage in his mind'.** Yet as the play progresses, the associations and qualities of black and blackness are less clear-cut.

Activity 8

Consider the ways in which references to black are used in the extracts below. How far do you agree with the view that Othello himself comes to accept blackness as a negative quality?

A From **'Haply for I am black…'** to **'Must be to loathe her'** (*Othello, Act 3, Scene 3*)

B From **'I'll have some proof…'** to **'As mine own face'** (*Othello, Act 3, Scene 3*)

C From **'Arise, black vengeance…'** to **'To tyrannous hate!'** (*Othello, Act 3, Scene 3*)

Role-playing and storytelling

The plot hinges upon the lies fed to Othello about his wife, and part of Shakespeare's structuring of the drama is to let us possess this knowledge from the beginning of the play. Iago confesses that he is playing a role. The theme of appearance and reality finds its expression in many of the other threads of the play and so, when you explore role-playing, it is difficult to see it as distinct from issues connected with deception, dishonesty and outward appearance.

The conscious adoption of a role is addressed in Act 1, Scene 1, when Iago confesses,'**I am not what I am**'. Shakespeare shows us this admission and then allows us to observe the ways in which Iago goes on to play this role. Iago could almost be interpreted as stage director – he seems to determine the roles that characters play and how they are interpreted, and yet he is an actor too, playing a role that brings about the tragic resolution.

The role Iago conjures up for Desdemona to play is not one she willingly adopts, but one forced upon her, and one Othello fails to see through. Men and women in the play are often forced into various roles as determined by the society they live in.

> **Key quotation**
>
> **And what's he then that says I play the villain,**
> **When this advice is free I give, and honest,**
> (*Iago, Act 2, Scene 3*)

Activity 9

Michael Cassio presents different faces to the women he encounters. Consider what the audience learns about Cassio in the extracts below. What conclusions do you come to about Cassio and the roles he might play in the world of the text?

A From **'O, behold…'** to **'Enwheel thee round'** (*Cassio, Act 2, Scene 1*)

B From **'I marry her?…'** to **'Ha, ha, ha!'**; from **'She was here even now…'** to **'… falls me thus about my neck'**; **''Tis such another fitchew! Marry, a perfumed one'** (*Cassio, Act 4, Scene 1*)

> ### Activity 10
>
> Iago's misogynistic observations about women in Act 2, Scene 1 also present women as role-players whose public face is different from the reality of their domestic personae. Read Act 2, Scene 1, from **'Come on, come on...'** to **'... and housewives in your beds'**. Then consider whether any of these roles are reflected in the actions and behaviour of Desdemona and Emilia.

Iago's ability to determine a role for Desdemona, albeit a false representation, is a form of storytelling. He constructs a narrative in which the victim is placed centrestage and made to act for Othello. In Act 4, Scene 1, Iago cunningly positions Othello in such a way that he misinterprets Cassio's words about Bianca and, in doing so, shapes the narrative that he, Iago, wants Othello to believe about his wife's conduct.

Storytelling is fiction. Even tales that have a basis in truth are only representations of events. Perhaps one of the interpretations of the play might be that it reveals how gullible humans are to trust in stories and how narrative itself is a seductive art that offers a unified version of the world, even if that version isn't the truth. The last two lines in the play, delivered by Lodovico, suggest that he will give a version of the events to the senate.

> ### Key quotation
>
> **Myself will straight aboard, and to the state**
> **This heavy act with heavy heart relate.**
> *(Lodovico, Act 5, Scene 2)*

Here are some of the stories told in the first act of the play.

- The play commences with a story being told to Brabantio about his daughter's elopement.
- Iago tells how he has slain men on the battlefield.
- Brabantio speculates a tale about Othello's seduction of his daughter.
- The senate hears Othello's account of how he fell in love with Desdemona.
- Othello has told stories to Brabantio and Desdemona about his early life.
- Iago sells Roderigo a story, suggesting he will win Desdemona's love.

> ### Activity 11
>
> Remind yourself of the events of Acts 2–5. In a table, note down as many instances you can of storytelling. Who tells these tales and to whom? Are their tales based on truth or lies?

Activity 12

In Act 1, Scene 3, from **'Wherein I spake of most disastrous chances…'** to **'Would Desdemona seriously incline'**, Othello explains the tales he has told to Desdemona about his earlier life. Consider the likely truth of this story and explore the view that Othello himself is little more than a storyteller. To what extent is Desdemona and Othello's love built on fictions?

Power, honour and honesty

The world of Venice and the army in which several of the male characters serve are places governed by rank and status. The senate conducts its business in a measured way, with the Duke providing strong, thoughtful leadership. It appears to respect the status of Brabantio and Othello. Yet issues of male power seem to be central to the narrative, driving the plot and raising the spectre of violence and confrontation.

Consider the disputes and power relationships that Act 1 introduces:

- Iago is manipulating Roderigo for financial gain.
- Iago and Roderigo are antagonizing the older father figure, Brabantio.
- Iago despises Cassio and is jealous of his higher status.
- Iago despises Othello for choosing Cassio as lieutenant.
- Brabantio and Othello are competing for 'ownership' of Desdemona.
- The Duke has the power to decide in the struggle for Desdemona.
- Desdemona stands up for her husband.
- Brabantio, the father figure, loses out to Othello.
- The less powerful Iago determines to unseat the general.

Activity 13

Track through the events of Acts 2–5. Which other male disputes emerge and how are they resolved?

Although the text generally suggests that women suffer at the hands of men, Emilia's observations to Desdemona in Act 4, Scene 3 are a plea for equality. Emilia's worldly take on male and female relationships appears cynical at times, but her speech offers a well-argued case for equal treatment. Emilia's attempt to speak at the end of the play results in her death, however.

Emilia (Leila Crerar) shares her philosophy with Desdemona (Kirsty Oswald), Lyric Hammersmith, 2015

Activity 14

Read Emilia's words, when she speaks to Desdemona in Act 4, Scene 3, from 'Let husbands know…' to '… their ills instruct us so'.

a) Write an explanation of Emilia's argument.

b) Is there any evidence in the text of the equality she calls for?

c) To what extent do you feel this play is an analysis of the damaging effects of male power and female subservience?

Key quotation

So please your grace, my ancient:
A man he is of honesty and trust
(Othello, Act 1, Scene 3)

Male honour, in terms of status and the fear of cuckoldry, is explored in the text. It might be argued that much of Othello's despair is about his loss of honour regarding Desdemona's apparent infidelity. Although he makes reference to her body being used by others, it seems that for the most part he is concerned with the implications that it brings upon him. The behaviour of females in the play, and also perhaps in the world itself, is often connected with honour. Sexual misbehaviour risked loss of reputation, and so courtesans like Bianca were judged to be merely sexual entertainment rather than material for marriage. Desdemona's reputation is sullied, which therefore brings Othello's honour into question and, by extension, his suitability for high office.

Activity 15

Othello's final speech before stabbing himself in Act 5, Scene 2, from **'Soft you…'** to **'And smote him thus'**, embodies many of the themes of the play. Re-read it and consider whether it:

- is a form of storytelling that fictionalizes the events of the play
- is an attempt to reconfigure the notion of honour and honesty through words and suicide
- confers some power back on Othello.

Activity 16

Read the following statements about thematic issues arising from the play. Consider the extent to which you agree with them.

A Jealousy in its various forms is the central theme of the play.

B Disorder is evident from the very beginning of the play. There are very few scenes that suggest an ordered, peaceful world.

C The play reveals the stupidity of male behaviour in regard to relationships with females.

D The play reveals the disastrous effects that male bravado and reputation has on females.

E Women in the text are always judged on their compliance or refusal to comply with the expectations placed upon them in terms of sexual conduct.

Writing about themes

Writing about themes and ideas is effective when you make links across the text and explore how themes are developed and added to as the story progresses. Being aware of how an idea is introduced, and then how it is repeated and expanded in later parts of the narrative is a useful way to bring together ideas about meanings and points about the playwright's method. *Othello* doesn't really have a subplot as such, but be alert to how a theme might be introduced mainly through one character's actions but is then mirrored through another character.

Other structural ideas such as contrast are useful starting points for illuminating work on themes. For instance, you might compare the ways in which the marriage between Othello and Desdemona contrasts with that of Iago and Emilia. You should also consider the extent to which themes such as power are explored in numerous contexts. Linking theme to backdrops such as gender, power and social matters are profitable ways to tie in work on both meaning and context.

Othello is a play that has generated many critical responses. The contentious but universal subject matter, and the changing contexts in which the play is performed and received, have ensured that *Othello* has a long critical history. Literary criticism and other academic responses to texts can illuminate your understanding of the play and help you view its content from different angles.

Activity 1

As a starting point for your study of critical views, explore some early responses to *Othello*. Find online versions of Thomas Rymer's 1693 assessment of the play and Samuel Taylor Coleridge's 1818 notes on the play.

What key points do Rymer and Coleridge make about the play?

Reading positions and approaches

Critical opinions about texts are personal responses, but they are never free from the cultural baggage and prejudices of the person who writes them. Although it is tempting to read critical opinion simply as a person's individual response, it embodies the ethical values of the person and society in which the response was written. The approach critics decide to adopt towards the text says a lot about what they think is the 'correct' or most illuminating way to read literature.

Essentialist criticism, an older approach that analysed characters as if they were 'real', has largely been overtaken by approaches that see literature as **representational criticism**. This means judging characters and texts as representations of society, and therefore the task of the reader/critic is to look at the representation that is offered in the text and to explore the ideology (view of the world) it proposes.

Two central approaches or schools of thought on how literature can be read are Marxist criticism and gender criticism.

Marxist criticism

This approach takes its cue from the political beliefs originating in the views of Karl Marx, an economist and philosopher. Adopting a Marxist approach to reading literature means exploring the representation of power, class and status in the world of the text. Marx's view was that economic situations determine everything in the real world. This means that analysing the interaction of social and economic factors in the text, and also the conditions in which the text was produced, is central to any reading.

Adopting a Marxist approach to reading literature also means acknowledging that human beings are less free than they might think and that what we might think of as 'the way the world works' is an illusion. The prevailing ideology is designed by those in power to keep them in power. The powerless, by contrast, see this ideology as 'common sense' and 'normal' rather than anything that could be challenged. Consequently, Marxist critics look closely at issues of conflict, ideology and class struggle in the world of the text.

essentialist criticism looking for the essence of a character itself, as if the character had a 'real' existence

representational criticism seeing characters and situations as constructs – versions of 'real' characters and events. Representational readings place emphasis on how they have been shown by the writer, and what they reveal about the values of society and the writer

Activity 2

Consider the role of power and status in the play. You could explore:

a) the role of the senate and how the political system is organized – and its values – in the Venice represented in the play

b) the power relations between Othello, Cassio and Iago. How far do status differences explain the actions of the characters?

c) whether Iago could be viewed positively as a repressed, powerless character who destroys the power structures that keep him in his place.

Gender criticism

This approach looks at the ways literature represents masculinity and femininity. Readers exploring texts from this angle take the view that literature can promote negative images of gender, helping to support stereotypes rather than challenge them. Females, for example, might be portrayed in narrow roles as virginal or whorish, helpless or shrewish. Exploring the depiction of both genders can reveal a lot about the way society and the writer views men and women.

There is an assumption that the general reader of a text is male and that the sorts of texts promoted by educational institutions are mainly the work of dead white males. Feminist critics explore and expose the view that to be male and heterosexual is 'normal' and to be female or gay is to be 'different'.

Activity 3

Consider the role of gender in the play. You could explore:

a) what masculinity means in the play. How much of it is bound up with toughness and power? Are men ever 'weak' in the text? If so, what happens to them?

b) whether females in the play are always victims. Are they always represented as powerless?

c) whether Emilia might be read positively as a woman who asserts herself and stands up to male power in the play.

Activity 4

There are many other critical theories and approaches that could inform your study of *Othello*. Some theoretical approaches are relatively new and still evolving. Some approaches are complex and demand careful study. Research the following areas and their potential usefulness to your reading of the play:

- post-colonialism
- narrative and narratology
- psychoanalytical
- eco-criticism
- postmodernism.

Beginning to apply critical views

As you begin to explore published critical views, take time to understand the arguments being proposed, the approach being taken and, crucially, whether you agree with what is being said. The extract below was written by John Wain in 1971 as part of the introduction to a selection of critical essays.

Activity 5

Read Text A, taking careful note of the main points of the argument, which have been highlighted.

a) Is the reading that the tragic outcome in *Othello* arises from misunderstanding a convincing argument?

b) Is the story of Iago one of revelation too? Is it possible to see Iago's character arc as a 'fall'?

Text A

Othello, as I saw it then and still see it now, is a tragedy of misunderstanding. No one among the characters understands anyone else; nor are they, for the most part, very strong on self-understanding either. If Othello understood Desdemona, he would know that she is simply not the kind of girl who would, during their very honeymoon, start a love affair with his first officer. If Desdemona understood Othello, she would know that he does not yet see her as a real girl, but as something magical that has happened to him, and that he will run mad if anything should happen to make him believe that her white magic has turned to black. If Emilia understood Iago she would know that he is not merely a coarsely domineering husband who has forced her into endless petty compromises for the sake of peace and a modus vivendi, but also, on a side hidden from her, a fiend who delights in torture. But then Iago does not, until it happens, know this about himself. Unaware of the power of love, he cannot imagine the suffering into which he will plunge Othello by plausibly slandering Desdemona, and therefore cannot imagine the holocaust at the end. Nor can he foresee the transformation that will occur in himself. The great temptation scene (III iii) is so convincing because it shows Iago's fall as well as Othello's. At the beginning of that scene they are both sane men; at the end, they are both mad, and both in the grip of the same madness.

(John Wain, 'Introduction', in *Shakespeare: Othello (Casebook Series)*, edited by John Wain. Palgrave Macmillan, 1994)

Interpreting Othello

In the following extracts from critical essays, each critic gives a slightly different emphasis on Othello, his actions and how they can be interpreted.

Activity 6

Texts B–D all examine how Othello's actions at the end of the play can be judged. Text B looks specifically at his final speech, whereas Texts C and D give judgements on Othello's moral and personal position.

Using Texts B–D, explore:

a) the differences between these readings in terms of how they judge Othello

b) what evidence in the play you can find to support or challenge the views given

c) which, if any, of the views is closest to your own.

Text B

What Othello seems to me to be doing in making this speech is cheering himself up. He is endeavouring to escape reality, he has ceased to think about Desdemona, and is thinking about himself. Humility is the most difficult of all virtues to achieve; nothing dies harder than the desire to think well of oneself. Othello succeeds in turning himself into a pathetic figure, by adopting an aesthetic rather than a moral attitude, dramatizing himself against his environment. He takes in the spectator, but the human motive is primarily to take in himself.

(T.S. Eliot, *Shakespeare and the Stoicism of Seneca,* 1927)

Text C

But Iago's victory is not absolute. During the last scene, Othello is a nobly tragic figure. His ravings are not final: he rises beyond them. He slays Desdemona finally not so much in rage, as for 'the cause' (V ii 1). He slays her in love. Though Desdemona fails him, his love, homeless, 'perplexed in the extreme' (V ii 345), endures. He will kill her and 'love her after' (V ii 19). In that last scene, too, he utters the grandest of his poetry. The Iago-spirit never finally envelops him, masters him, disintegrates his soul.

(G. Wilson Knight, *The Othello Music,* 1930)

Text D

At this climax of the play, as he sets himself irrevocably in his vindictive resolution, he reassumes formally his heroic self-dramatization – reassumes the Othello of 'the big wars that make ambition virtue'. The part of this conscious nobility, this noble egotism, this self-pride that was justified by experience irrelevant to the present trials and stresses, is thus underlined. Othello's self-idealization, his promptness to jealousy and his blindness are shown in their essential relation. The self-idealization is shown as blindness and the nobility as here no longer something real, but the disguise of an obtuse and brutal egotism. Self-pride becomes stupidity, ferocious stupidity, an insane and self-deceiving passion. The habitual 'nobility' is seen to make self-deception invincible, the egotism it expresses being the drive to catastrophe. Othello's noble lack of self-knowledge is shown as humiliating and disastrous.

(F.R. Leavis, *Diabolic Intellect and the Noble Hero,* 1952)

Interpreting Iago

Activity 7

Read Iago's lines from **'I would not have your free and noble nature...'** to **'... but keep't unknown'** *(Act 3, Scene 3)*. Then read Text E, which gives a reading of Iago's manipulation and power over Othello.

a) Consider how far you agree with the highlighted comments.

b) Prepare your counter-argument to this text in which you argue that Iago's 'strategy of separation' is not, in fact, the most crucial strategy he employs.

" **Text E**

[In lines 201–06] Iago introduces Othello to the idea that acting is a basic practice of Venetian society manners. [...]

Of all Iago's strategies of separation this is the most crucial, for it moves Othello into an area of which he has neither knowledge nor experience where the certain truth he seeks is, by definition, elusive. We are inclined not to impute simple gullibility to Othello as the cause of his fall because of the way everyone trusts Iago's honesty. But there are more particular reasons why Othello, who is induced to distrust Venetians, can nevertheless trust Iago. The ensign is, in the manner that Othello thinks of himself, a rough, blunt-spoken soldier who has lived on battlefields where the sophisticated role playing of civilian society has little opportunity to flourish. Iago is a man without polish more to be relished in the soldier than in the scholar.

(Anthony Brennan, 'Iago, The Strategist of Separation', in *Shakespeare's Dramatic Structures*, Routledge, 2013) "

'... now I shall have reason to show the love and duty that I bear you', says 'honest' Iago; Christopher Obi (left) and Michael Mueller (right), 2010 Ludlow Festival

Interpreting tragedy

In these next two pieces of criticism, the writers explore the nature of the tragedy and how it can be viewed. Read Texts F and G carefully and consider whether:

a) the tragedy in the play is universal in nature, as Text F claims

b) any of the aspects of the play might be deemed 'comic'

c) whether the view that the play is a **farce** is convincing.

Text F

Othello is eminently a domestic tragedy. But this element in the play is yet to be related to another more universal element. Othello is concretely human, so is Desdemona. Othello is very much the typical middle-aged bachelor entering matrimony late in life, but he is also, to transpose a phrase of Iago's, a symbol of human – especially masculine – 'purpose, courage, and valour' (IV ii 218), and, in a final judgement, is seen to represent the idea of human faith and value in a very wide sense. Now Desdemona, also very human, with an individual domestic feminine charm and simplicity, is yet also a symbol of woman in general daring the unknown seas of marriage with the mystery of man.

(G .Wilson Knight,*The Othello Music*,1930)

Text G

Othello brings us face to face with the problem not elsewhere encountered in the tragedies, or indeed in Shakespeare's works in general: the distinction between tragic and comic. Normally the question doesn't arise. But it does here, because, to paraphrase Horace Walpole's mot, the play is tragic if we can feel a part of it, comic if we look at it from the outside. And the distinction, like all such distinctions where Othello is concerned, is very absolute and abrupt. Nothing could be more surprising, in a way, than to find a tension between comic and tragic treatment suddenly making itself felt. And it was sensed early on. Writing at the end of the same century in which Othello was first produced Thomas Rymer called the play 'a [...] farce'.

(John Bayley, 'Tragedy and Consciousness: Othello', in *Shakespeare and Tragedy*. Routledge, 1981)

farce a comic dramatic work including crude characterization and ridiculously improbable situations

Interpreting narrative

Rather than focus upon character or theme, some criticism looks at the way in which texts are structured and the effects that are generated. Text H looks at how the playwright controls the flow of knowledge within the play as opposed to the audience's awareness.

Activity 9

Read Text H and consider:

a) what information the audience possesses that the characters do not possess

b) which events in the play are the most tense in terms of the audience's response.

Text H

In tragedy the audience is often given knowledge that is denied to the characters. Because the audience is not subject to clouded judgement by participation in the action, it has the freedom to understand why catastrophe must occur and must watch helplessly while the characters use their freedom and proceed in ignorance to make assurance of death double sure. This burden of special knowledge with which the playwright invests his audience can be exploited in a great variety of ways. The tension experienced by the audience can be tuned to an almost unbearable level when the audience feels that the characters are ensnared in a trick of plot which simple information could dispel. Many of Shakespeare's tragedies, however, do not aim to produce a sense of helpless frustration in the audience at its inability to interfere in the course of events.

(A. Brennan, 'Iago, The Strategist of Separation', in *Shakespeare's Dramatic Structures*, Routledge, 2013)

Interpreting symbols

Another type of narrative-based criticism involves looking at how symbols and motifs, such as the handkerchief, might be read.

Activity 10

Read Text I carefully.

a) Explore the idea that the 'hypocritical virtue' can be credibly applied to Desdemona.

b) Explore whether the handkerchief can be seen as representative of Desdemona's body and what this might mean in terms of gender and power in the text.

Emilia (Maeve Larkin) and Iago (Conrad Nelson) play out a power struggle over the handkerchief, Northern Broadsides and West Yorkshire Playhouse, 2009

 Text I

The handkerchief in Othello […] accumulates myriad associations and meanings. It first appears simply as a love token given by Othello to Desdemona and therefore treasured by her; only later do we learn the details of its provenance and design. In the Renaissance, strawberries signified virtue or goodness, but also hypocritical virtue as symbolized by the frequently occurring design and emblem of a strawberry plant with an adder hiding beneath its leaves.

(Karen Newman, '"And wash the Ethiop White": Femininity and the Monstrous in Othello', in *Fashioning Femininity and English Renaissance Drama*, 2009)

Developing your own readings

Critical views are useful in provoking thought and inviting you to look at the play from different angles. They should be exercised with caution and engaged with, rather than taken as 'correct' viewpoints. The most important view of the play's elements is your own. Any response you give to the play will be ultimately your own views, although it may well be informed by those of other readers and published critical opinions.

Part of the process of generating your own opinion of the play may be helped by applying the two different reading approaches mentioned at the start of this chapter. Although there are different types of gender and Marxist criticism, considering how these sorts of approaches might make you see the play in different ways can be a useful starting point.

Activity 11

Re-read Act 4, Scene 3, from **'My mother had a maid called Barbary...'** to **'Hark, who is't that knocks?'** Consider how different reading approaches might help you generate views about this part of the play.

a) Explore the representations of gender in this extract. What significant aspects of masculinity and femininity are shown here? What is the balance of power between male and female? Is it possible to say that familiar stereotypes of women are employed?

b) Look closely at the nature of power and status here, especially between Desdemona and Emilia. What is shown about the way social structures operate here? Although she occupies a lesser social status in the world of the text, do Emilia's actions and words reflect this?

c) How does the use of song and references to nature and the past contribute to the meanings of the play? What might be said about the ways in which the relationship between females and nature is shown here?

Writing about critical views

When you read criticism in conjunction with *Othello*, you are effectively juggling two texts. Critical views are essentially writing about writing and are, in the end, just views. Rather than taking a critical view at face value, it is important that you first of all understand what is being said and that you then evaluate it. Read criticism *critically*. You should test views out and see if you agree with them – or not. Never just refer to a view. Look at the strengths and weaknesses of the reading.

Exam skills

Writing about any literary text involves a set of key skills that you will need to practise and master. Insightful, effective responses about any piece of literature are grounded in your understanding of the text. During the course of your studies, you must ensure that you are confident about the plot, structure, characters, settings, themes and genre elements of *Othello*. This will enable you to select wisely the material you want to focus on, ensuring you choose the most fruitful aspects of the text to explore in your writing.

Whether you set your own questions or respond to tasks given to you, writing about *Othello* at A/AS level requires you to work on your phrasing skills, take account of dramatic method, context and genre, and, most importantly, focus closely on the question you are presented with. Invariably, A/AS level tasks will ask more specific questions, sometimes offering debates to respond to or an extract to comment on. The quality of your ideas, the strength of your argument and your own personal voice will be central to any piece of writing you construct. Refining your thinking and discussion skills will undoubtedly aid your writing.

Focusing on the task

Questions, or tasks as they are often termed, require an answer. The wording of a task is carefully crafted to stimulate your thoughts and point you in certain directions. Ignoring the task and simply writing 'everything I know about the play' will result in a poor essay. Similarly, taking a question and 'warping' it so you can write about what you know best (rather than answering the actual question you've been given) will also have a disastrous outcome. Focusing on the task in hand, and looking at the key words in the question, is the starting point of an effective answer.

Activity 1

Look carefully at the following task. What are the key words? What precisely is the task inviting you to do?

> How far do you agree that Shakespeare presents Othello as heroic and admirable?

The first thing you might have noticed is the invitation to offer an opinion. This is carried in the words: 'How far do you agree…'. The use of the second person pronoun should alert you to the fact that this type of task is asking for *your* opinion. It is therefore important that your response does provide *your* opinion and, you must come to a conclusion.

The first five words also tell you that there is some sort of debate being set up. There are two strands to the debate: the first opinion you are given to react to is the view that Othello is 'heroic' and then, allied to that, the view that he is 'admirable'. It is possible to take issue or support one or both of these readings of the protagonist, so any effective essay will need to work very closely with these key terms and build an argument around them.

You will also have recognized that the term 'heroic' introduces both a literary and a cultural concept – that of heroism. In literature, the notion of a hero is sometimes used to signify a protagonist, or agent of the text. A literary hero usually engenders the reader's sympathy and has positive qualities that go some way to helping them achieve their aim in the narrative of the text.

When used in relation to *Othello*, the term 'heroic' may also bring to mind some generic context – that of the tragic hero. As a cultural term, 'heroic' suggests worthy of admiration or brave, perhaps. You should be aware that the word may well mean a variety of things to different audiences, but here, your cultural concept of what a hero is should be the one you work with. Perhaps it might be worth defining what your understanding of the two key terms are before you begin to plan an answer.

Another aspect of the task is carried in the words 'Shakespeare presents'. Here you are being reminded that there is a playwright, who carefully shapes and arranges the material. Othello is not a real person; he is a conscious construct. You are being asked to look at how the playwright structures the text: what he has Othello doing, the key moments he is involved in, the use of soliloquy, his character arc, the words used, etc. Remember that writing about method doesn't mean writing *anything* about method: it must be relevant to the task.

So, in summary, the task requires you to debate the ideas that Othello is heroic and admirable, and to think about Shakespeare's methods as you do so. Implicit in all of this are the assumptions that you will write clearly and fluently, and use evidence – quotations or references – to support your points.

Some reminders

Writing effective essays shouldn't be reduced to a checklist. Formulaic responses run the risk of being straitjacketed, rather than interesting and creative. It is possible, however, to use the following prompts to judge the quality of your own work.

- How closely do I focus on the key terms in the task?
- How well do I get involved in the debate?
- What is the quality of my argument? How convincing is it?
- Is my essay well structured and fluently written?
- Do I write relevantly about Shakespeare's method?

Activity 2

Using the prompt list above, read the following sample student responses and judge the quality of each answer. They are all partial answers to the following task:

> How far do you agree that Shakespeare presents Othello as heroic and admirable?

Sample answer 1

In Act I, Othello stands accused of ensnaring Desdemona by witchcraft, a charge he denies. It is clear that Desdemona loves him and, when they travel to Cyprus separately and are reunited, it is clear that their union is strong and they are happy in each other's company. Othello is a well-respected general and he goes to Cyprus to defend Venice. Othello seems happy for a while but Iago plots against him and, gradually, Othello and his wife are divided through jealousy. He thinks his wife is sleeping with Cassio. Othello has strong physical reactions to Iago's insinuations: he falls into a trance, strikes his wife and eventually smothers her. It is clear that Othello is a victim, and his final speech and act of suicide are a way of acknowledging his crimes.

Sample answer 2

Like most tragic heroes, Othello possesses noble qualities in the initiation phase of the narrative: Shakespeare gives him a certain stature – that of military hero and dignified man placed in a strange setting. His poetic speeches reference 'Olympus', 'Hellespont' and 'plumed troops', which all lend a heroic prestige to the protagonist. His flinty acceptance of his posting to Cyprus suggests heroism, yet he is more of a tragic hero – a character trapped by the machinations of Iago and, perhaps, by his own shortcomings. Unlike most literary heroes, Othello dies after smothering his own wife. It's debatable whether it is possible to admire Othello at all: he is perhaps more of a victim than a hero and his treatment of Desdemona makes him impossible to categorize as 'admirable'.

As you read the student responses, you will have noticed both are written in clear English and show understanding of the play and its events. But you will hopefully have noticed that the second response is better. Re-read the responses in conjunction with the following commentaries.

Sample answer 1 doesn't really focus on the debate at the heart of the question. Instead, it gives an overview of what Othello does in the play and reads more like a plot summary than an answer to a specific task. It is very difficult to see where the answer does connect with the question, but there are echoes of 'heroic' when it mentions Othello being a 'well-respected general' and it might be that the statement that Othello is 'acknowledging his crimes' is very indirectly suggesting admirable qualities. Otherwise, the grasp on the question is weak. There is little sense of dramatic method being tackled here, although the answer acknowledges how the play commences and ends. The answer tends to treat the character as a real person and never once refers to how Shakespeare structures the material. Although the response is written clearly, there are no quotations used.

Sample answer 2 takes a wider view of the task and immediately places the protagonist against the generic backdrop of tragedy. There is an acknowledgement of Othello's nobility and a sharp sense of Shakespeare's method – the shape of the story and references to setting and language too. Interesting quotations are chosen and everything is tethered to the question. There is a very good grasp of what heroism constitutes, with some interesting points made about stature and dignity. What distinguishes this as a very good answer is the focus on the debate. The term 'hero' is taken issue with and refined with, once again, reference to genre. An interesting idea is proposed – that Othello is more of a victim than a hero. A strong personal voice emerges, with a strident dismissal of the idea that the protagonist is admirable. The writing is fluent and the quality of argument strong.

Activity 3

Write your own paragraph to the task you explored above. Choose different examples to those used in Sample answer 2 to support your own view.

Planning and structuring an answer

At A/AS level, planning and thinking before you write becomes even more important. A coherent, well-structured response does not happen unless some degree of forethought occurs. As you saw above, focusing closely upon the key terms and structuring an answer around them is vital. Once you've identified the point of the task, it makes sense to do the following:

1. Think carefully about the whole narrative of the play. Which parts of it – which events and scenes – are going to be most useful in helping you to answer the task? If you are engaging with a debate, are there parts of the play that show the character or theme in different lights?

2. Jot down a list of points you wish to make, ensuring that every one serves the question. Resist any temptation to show off knowledge that is not relevant to the question.

3. Choose some quotations to employ in the body of the essay.

4. Work out a 'route through' your essay. It may well be that in a debate-style task, you might want to commence by looking at the main view proposed in the task, and then move on to alternative views.

5. Work out what your conclusion would be. Your conclusion needs to be a strong statement, which gives your definitive answer to the task. The best writing is often committed to a certain view, but acknowledges the contrasting or conflicting elements of the debate.

6. Use your conclusion to help you write your introduction.

Writing convincing introductions

A good introduction should signpost an argument. Ideally, the person who reads your work should be able to get a sense of what your argument is going to be. If you plan your answer properly and know what your conclusion will be, then you can signal it in your introduction.

Activity 4

Compare the following two introductions. Which is the more effective, and why?

> How far do you agree that Shakespeare presents Othello as heroic and admirable?

Student A

Othello was written in 1604 and tells the story of a heroic general and how he falls from grace, murdering his wife by the end of the narrative. Shakespeare bases the story on an older tale known as Cinthio's Story, but changes some key parts in order to refocus the story on Othello rather than his wife. The word 'heroic' means brave and 'admirable' means worthy of respect. In this essay, I will debate whether Othello is heroic and admirable, and come to some conclusions about it.

Student B

In 'Othello' Shakespeare presents a complex protagonist whose heroic actions are brought into question by his less-than-admirable actions in the latter end of the play. While the noble Othello of Act I may well deserve the epithet 'admirable', the tragedy only makes full sense if we understand that Shakespeare is trying to show the audience how initially heroic, admirable characters (even powerful generals) are susceptible to human frailty. By the end of the play, it is not accurate to deem Othello either 'heroic' or 'admirable'.

Choosing quotations

One of the arts you need to master is that of selection. In a play containing many memorable lines, being able to select the most telling, relevant quotation to help you clinch a point is essential. Quotations may only be a few words in length, but should be judiciously chosen. Lengthy quotations often get in the way of a good point. Embed short quotations within the body of your paragraphs, using them as ways to sum up a point or as a springboard to move on.

Activity 5

Re-read Act 5, Scene 2, from **'A better never did itself sustain…'** to **'And fiends will snatch at it'**. If you were required to answer the task on Othello as a 'heroic and admirable' character, which lines or phrases from this scene would you select to support or challenge the view given? What would your arguments be?

Activity 6

Using the skills you have practised so far, plan an answer to the following task.

> To what extent do you agree that in *Othello* Shakespeare presents jealousy as a merely ridiculous feeling?

You should:

a) select the most relevant parts of the text to write about

b) work out what your argument would be

c) select useful quotations

d) make a list of the points you would make, in order

e) write a coherent introduction and conclusion.

Activity 7

Now write an answer to the task you have planned in Activity 6.

Sample answers

Read Sample answers 1 and 2, which are extracts from two student responses to the question you planned in Activity 6. Then read the annotations and concluding commentary on each response.

Then compare the essay you wrote in Activity 7 to the sample answers. Is it more like Sample answer 1 or 2? How might you set about improving your response?

Sample answer 1

To what extent do you agree that in *Othello* Shakespeare presents jealousy as a merely ridiculous feeling?

Undoubtedly, the actions brought about by jealousy, and the irrational behaviour exhibited by the characters who succumb to that destructive emotion in the play, do suggest that jealousy produces absurd, faintly ridiculous effects. There is a child-like aspect to the manner in which Othello, a leading general, is so wound up by his emotions that he resorts to gnashing his teeth, fainting and superstition. Yet to say that the manifestation of jealousy in the play simply has the effect of producing mild comedy is to miss the point of the text: Shakespeare quite clearly structures the text to show the absolute tragedy that results from 'the green-eyed monster'. It is very difficult to ignore the fact that death results from jealousy. Far from showing jealousy to be merely a ridiculous feeling, Shakespeare shows its corrosive qualities and reminds us all that, regardless of power and status, human weakness brings tragic outcomes.

The theme of jealousy is introduced in the first lines of the play: Shakespeare clearly wishes the audience to see its importance to the overall meanings of the narrative. Rather than Othello, however, it is Iago's professional jealousy that is first drawn to the audience's attention. In Act 1, Scene 1, displeased with Cassio's promotion, Iago states 'I know my price, I am worth no worse a place'. There appear to be some juvenile feelings here and it is possible to see the ridiculous aspect of such an opinion. Iago, a grown soldier, is so incensed that he belittles Cassio, claiming 'Mere prattle without practice is all his soldiership'. His bitterness at this 'counter-caster' seems like sour grapes and may well be read as ridiculous.

Iago's jealousy is partly sexual – he says of Desdemona, 'I do love her too'. He also suspects Othello 'hath leapt into my seat'. There is no real indication that Othello and Emilia have been unfaithful though and it

Addresses the task directly, clearly grasps the point of the task and offers some agreement with the main view set up in the task.

Gives more details in support of the main view but, crucially, signposts the counter-argument. The writing is purposeful and a strong opinion is evident. An apt quotation is used for support.

Widens out the debate and links to the tragic context of the play. By the end of the introduction, the scope of the debate has been grasped and there is a sense that the argument is being set up in fluent English.

Expands the main view in the task – that jealousy is faintly ridiculous. Gives useful supporting references and there is awareness of Shakespeare's crafting of the story.

is certainly true that Desdemona is guiltless. Taken together, we have a play in which sexual jealousy is completely misplaced and so, for death to result from an error of judgement or a deliberate lie, it can seem ridiculous indeed. Additionally, the sight of Venice's leading general falling into a trance or being misled by the questionable proof of a strawberry-spotted handkerchief is vaguely ridiculous too.

Develops the counter-argument. Uses several well-chosen quotations to show how jealousy is destructive. There is a good sense of Shakespeare's method here too.

It is, however, impossible to judge jealousy in the play as merely ridiculous. The ramifications of it are far from comic. Shakespeare designs the play so we see how one man's jealousy in turn causes another's, and the eventual effect is tragic. Jealousy has the ability to unseat a man's reason. Othello himself acknowledges that 'Chaos is come again', and Iago's ironic warning to the Moor that jealousy 'doth mock the meat it feeds on' is an apt description of the corrosive effects of passion.

Brings in wider contextual issues: introduces the backdrop of gender and employs further well-selected references.

Shows good awareness of how dramatic irony creates meaning in these lines.

As the play progresses, various key events show the increasingly destructive result of jealousy: the 'green-eyed monster' makes Othello strike his wife, deem her 'impudent strumpet' and torment himself with images in which 'the general camp, Pioners and all, had tasted her sweet body'. Othello's self-image is destroyed in the process – he fears he is cuckolded and his sense of his own masculinity, closely bound up with the sexual conduct of his wife, is challenged. Various negative sexual terms, such as 'impudent whore', are inaccurately applied to Desdemona. Her virtue is stained and, because Shakespeare structures his material so the audience are aware of Othello's mistaken beliefs and Desdemona's innocence, we are acutely aware of the injustice of it all.

Gives a confident conclusion and uses appropriate quotations to drive the argument home.

As the audience watches Desdemona breathe her last, innocently commending herself 'to my kind lord', and observes Othello's moment of recognition ('This look of thine will hurl my soul from heaven'), it is impossible to see the effects of jealousy as merely ridiculous. There is a recognizably human tragedy played out in the text, which shows that jealousy is a universal human emotion. It is also an incredibly destructive one.

Taken together, this response is highly effective: it focuses on the task very closely and the argument feels convincing. References are used well, with a good awareness of Shakespeare's method. The personal voice comes through in the writing, which is committed and fluently written. There are some links to genre and other contexts.

Sample answer 2

> To what extent do you agree that in *Othello* Shakespeare presents jealousy as a merely ridiculous feeling?

In 'Othello' jealousy is the central theme. Many of the characters are jealous – Iago is jealous of Cassio's appointment, Brabantio is jealous of Othello's acquisition of Desdemona and Othello is wrongly jealous of Desdemona's supposed affair.

Some focus on the question. Identifies different examples of jealousy yet there is no engagement with the debate yet.

If I was Othello, I am sure I'd have fallen into the same trap. Iago was very effective at manipulating Othello and introducing jealousy. Iago himself is jealous and says that Cassio is a 'spinster' and 'arithmetician'. The type of jealousy here is professional rather than sexual. But Iago is also in love with Desdemona and so he has other reasons to be jealous of Othello.

Seems a bit clumsy and treats the characters as if they are real.

Focuses on jealousy but still no real attempt to explore the debate. Text references are not too useful and seem only loosely linked to the task.

It is funny how all of the characters are jealous – it's a bit ridiculous how they all seem to want what they can't have. There are some funny parts, for example when Othello shouts and faints. This makes him appear weak, even though he's a general. It's also funny when the clown and Desdemona misunderstand each other in their pun-filled conversation.

Identifies different types of jealousy but, as elsewhere, there is no sense of Shakespeare's method.

It's not always ridiculous, though, especially when Desdemona is smothered and Othello kills himself. This proves that jealousy is a 'green-eyed monster' that harms people. The word 'green' has connotations of envy. I would say that jealousy in 'Othello' is sometimes ridiculous and sometimes serious, it just depends on who's reading it.

Engages with the debate but on a fairly superficial level. Uses basic examples without specific references.

Does not link to jealousy.

Brings in a counter-argument and a relevant quotation. Attempts to look at language but the point made is a simple one.

Avoids giving an answer and the essay ends weakly.

This response operates at a simple level. There is some focus on the debate but no real depth to the argument. For the most part, the characters are written about as if they are real people. There is little awareness of Shakespeare as the constructor of the text and no links made to genre or other context. The writing style, while clear, lacks flair.

Writing about extracts

There may be times when you are required to write in detail about a particular section of the text, so it is important that you are aware of the skills you need to practise for this.

Unlike a traditional essay, an extract task directs you to a specific moment in the play as the place to begin your answer. Yet it is essential that you look closely at the accompanying task because you will not be asked to write a running commentary on the extract. Instead, a debate or opinion is likely to be offered and your job is to use the extract as a starting point to explore that debate or opinion. Extract tasks invariably require you to broaden out your answer to the rest of the play, making links between the content of the extract and what happens elsewhere in the story.

When you are presented with an extract, you might consider some of the following questions before you begin to frame an answer.

- Where in the play does the extract come from? What has happened in the previous scene? What happens in the next scene?
- What is happening in the extract? What is the plot outline?
- Which characters appear in the extract? Who has most lines? Are any characters on stage but silent?
- Where is the scene set? Is there anything to be said about stage directions?
- Is this a scene where action is important or is it a 'quiet' scene where the reflections of the characters are more important?
- How does the extract commence? Is there anything significant about the first line?
- How does the extract end? Is there anything significant about the last line?
- How is dialogue used? Is there a soliloquy?
- What major themes are explored in the extract?
- Does this extract introduce a new character or theme?
- Are earlier events echoed in the extract?
- Does the extract have any bearing on the end of the play?
- Does this extract change your mind about any of the characters?

Once you have made notes on the general direction and point of the extract, turn your attention to the task. As ever, identify the debate or opinion at the heart of the task. Here are some specific things you could do:

- Underline the key terms in the task and make concrete links between the terms and the content of the extract.
- Re-read the extract, highlighting key pieces of dialogue/quotations that link with the task.

- Begin to frame your argument, making a list of clear points you would make in your answer.
- Consider the rest of the play and how it links to the extract in terms of character or theme. Select parts of the play/quotations that will illuminate your answer, or ones that might provide you with an alternative view.
- Work on your concluding point. What is your central argument/opinion?

Activity 9

Use the following task to help you refine your ability to write about extracts.

In Act 1, Scene 2, the audience already knows that Iago is plotting Othello's downfall. At the end of the previous scene, Brabantio has set off to apprehend Othello.

> Explore the ways Shakespeare presents the relationship between Iago and Othello in Act 1, Scene 2, from **'Though in the trade of war I have slain men...'** to **'By Janus, I think no'**. To what extent does it reflect their relationship in the remainder of the play?

a) Read the task and extract carefully, then plan an answer.

b) Once you have made a plan, draft an introduction and conclusion.

Activity 10

Before you look at a sample response, look closely at your plan and identify your own strengths and areas for development. Use these prompts to help you:

- How closely have I focused on the debate/opinion set up in the task?
- What do I intend to say about method, context and genre?
- How much do I plan to say about other parts of the play?
- How fluent and effective is my introduction and conclusion?

Activity 11

Read the first half of the following sample response to the question, taking note of the points made.

Sample answer 3, first half

> Explore the ways Shakespeare presents the relationship between Iago
> and Othello in Act 1, Scene 2, from **'Though in the trade of war I have
> slain men...'** to **'By Janus, I think no'**. To what extent does it reflect
> their relationship in the remainder of the play?

Prior to the start of this scene, the audience has already been exposed to Iago's complaints about his supposed mistreatment and already knows that Iago wishes to 'serve my turn upon him'. Shakespeare's use of dramatic irony means that by the time we see Iago and Othello together in this extract, we are aware that Iago is plotting Othello's downfall. Crucially, Othello is unaware of this. In the previous scene, Iago has provoked Brabantio's anger but claims to have come to help do him service. This backstory helps us understand how duplicitous Iago is, because in Act 1, Scene 2 (the first time we see the pair together), it appears that the villainous Ensign is aiding Othello.

The nature of their relationship in this extract is interesting because, on the surface, it appears that there is a sense of equality between the two, in spite of rank and status differences. Iago has little qualms about advising his general ('You were best go in') and has the lion's share of the dialogue at the start of the extract. Shakespeare commences the scene by having Iago express his defence of his general against Brabantio's accusations, claiming he would have 'yerked him here, under the ribs'. There is a great irony in his protestation that he lacks 'iniquity [...] to do me service', when it becomes quite clear later that he possesses enough malice to bring about several deaths by the end of the play. Othello, for his part, fails to see what the audience sees and that remains the case for a great deal of the play.

There is a sense that Iago is already playing with Othello's mind and putting some pressure upon him with regard to his marriage, suggesting that Brabantio will 'divorce you, Or put upon [...] restraint'. Yet at this point in the story, Shakespeare foregrounds Othello's nobility and measured approach. He seems firmly in command here, dismissing Iago's concerns ('Let him do his spite' and 'Not I; I must be found'). So it seems in this extract that Othello is in control of this relationship.

There is also a glimpse of the trust and confidences that Othello shares with his Ensign: personal matters are clearly shared. Othello's free admission 'I love the gentle Desdemona' suggests a bond between the two men and also a hint of danger – Othello clearly misplaces his trust in Iago and this has fatal consequences. The concluding oath offered by Iago ('By Janus') suggests the two-faced nature of the speaker of these words and yet, while the audience sees the allusions to deceit, Othello never does.

115

Activity 12

Sample answer 3 makes the following points about Othello and Iago's relationship in the extract. Locate these points in the sample answer:

a) Othello is unable to see Iago's manipulative behaviour.

b) There appears to be a sense of equality between them in spite of status differences.

c) Iago attempts to manipulate Othello.

d) Othello seems to be in control of the relationship.

e) There is obviously a bond that goes beyond a simple military relationship.

Activity 13

The second part of the task asks you to consider to what extent the relationship of the two men as presented in the extract reflects their relationship in the rest of the play.

Write the second half of this response, looking closely at how the power balance, trust and manipulative aspects of Iago and Othello's relationship develop in the remainder of the play.

Activity 14

Use the following task to help you practise your ability to write about extracts. Read the task and extract carefully, then write an answer.

In Act 1, Scene 1, Iago and Roderigo have arrived at Brabantio's house to inform him that Desdemona has married Othello. Brabantio is speaking from a high window to Iago and Roderigo in the street below.

Explore the ways Shakespeare presents conflict in Act 1, Scene 1, from 'Are your doors lock'd?' to '... you'll have coursers for cousins, and jennets for germans'. How are conflicts presented and resolved in the rest of the play?

Sample questions

1
Consider the idea that Desdemona is the most sympathetic character in the play.

2
Write about the different types of passions in the play, giving examples and commenting on how Shakespeare presents these emotions.

3
A reviewer commented that *Othello* is 'the saddest of all Shakespeare's plays'. What, if anything, do you find particularly sad about *Othello*?

4
'It is impossible to understand Iago's motives.' How far do you agree with this view?

5
Explore the tragic elements of *Othello*, using examples to demonstrate these features. What are the key events which lead to the tragic ending?

6
How far do you agree with the view that Iago is solely to blame for the negative events of the play?

Writing answers

One of the most important elements of your response is phrasing. As well as taking time to select quotations and build an argument, you should also take time to work on your written expression. At the very least, you need to write with clarity – ensure there are no vague sentences or sections in which your point is obscured by inexact wording.

Reading widely is the best way to improve your phrasing. The more texts you access, the more sentence constructions and individual words you will encounter and adapt for your own purposes. Literary criticism has a certain style, so the more academic writing you read, including journals, study guides, critical magazines and essays, the more you will get a feel for the voice of literary criticism. Broaden your reading by accessing broadsheet newspapers online and reading novels slightly beyond your comfort zone. Listen to spoken radio programmes and engage in discussion with other students when possible.

Above all, craft your writing. Draft and redraft your phrasing until it conveys precisely what you want it to say.

Glossary

abstract noun an idea, quality or state; something that does not exist as a material object

anagnorisis the moment of recognition when the protagonist realizes the significance of their mistakes

antagonist a character, often a villain, who stands in opposition to the main character

archetype a typical example; the original model or pattern of something

aside lines spoken directly by a character to the audience, which other onstage characters don't hear

backstory events that have happened before the play begins

bawdy humour comedy based on sexual or indecent content

catastrophe the climactic moment, usually the darkest moment in the play

catharsis the emotional release felt by the audience; a sense of cleansing

character arc the progress and development of a character during the text

comic relief an event or dialogue in a scene that releases tension through humour

complication an event that intensifies an existing conflict

concrete noun a thing you can experience through the use of your five senses (touch, taste, smell, sight, hearing)

dialogue the words spoken between characters

dramatic irony where the audience possesses more knowledge than the characters about events unfolding on stage

dramatic tragedy a play that shows the downfall and suffering of the protagonist, usually a person of great stature

essentialist criticism looking for the essence of a character itself, as if the character had a 'real' existence

euphemistic using an indirect or vague expression in place of a blunt or offensive observation

falling action sequence of events after the climax but before the resolution

farce a comic dramatic work including crude characterization and ridiculously improbable situations

figurative language figures of speech such as metaphor and simile

foregrounding making something stand out

hamartia a mistake made by the protagonist, which leads to their downfall

hubris excessive pride, which leads characters to ignore warnings and presume that they know best

imagery the use of visual or other vivid language to convey ideas

iamb two syllables comprising an unstressed and a stressed syllable

iambic pentameter a rhythm, a line composed of five iambs

ironically from irony, implying a secondary meaning, often revealing the truth of a situation

Machiavellian cunning, scheming and interested in selfish gain; derived from Niccolò Machiavelli's book *The Prince*

metaphor a figure of speech describing a person or thing by comparing them with something that is not literally applicable

metaphysical abstract or non-physical

motif a physical or metaphorical item that recurs in a text, taking on a range of meanings

peripeteia a catastrophe undergone by the protagonist; a reversal of fortune

polysyllabic consisting of several syllables

protagonist the central character, sometimes (but not always) a heroic figure

pun a double meaning; humour based on wordplay

representational criticism seeing characters and situations as constructs – versions of 'real' characters and events. Representational readings place emphasis on how they have been shown by the writer, and what they reveal about the values of society and the writer

resolution the final part of the story, in which a problem is resolved

simile a figure of speech comparing one thing with another of a different kind, using 'like' or 'as'

soliloquy a speech delivered by a character alone on stage

symbol an object that represents someone or something else

symbolism the use of an object that represents someone or something else

theme an idea that recurs throughout a story

OXFORD
UNIVERSITY PRESS

Great Clarendon Street, Oxford, OX2 6DP, United Kingdom

Oxford University Press is a department of the University of Oxford. It furthers the University's objective of excellence in research, scholarship, and education by publishing worldwide. Oxford is a registered trade mark of Oxford University Press in the UK and in certain other countries

British Library Cataloguing in Publication Data

Data available

ISBN 978-019-839898-1

Kindle edition ISBN 978-019-839899-8

10 9 8 7 6 5 4 3 2 1

Printed in Great Britain by CPI Group (UK) Ltd., Croydon CR0 4YY

Acknowledgements
The publisher and authors would like to thank the following for permission to use photographs and other copyright material:

Cover: © Paul Knight/Trevillion Images; **p9:** United Archives GmbH/Alamy Stock Photo; **p12:** theatrepix/Alamy Stock Photo; **p16:** Geraint Lewis/REX/Shutterstock; **p22, 25:** Donald Cooper/Photostage; **p29:** Heritage Images/Getty Images; **p33:** PHAS/Getty Images; **p34:** "Go to the Wars", illustration from a pamphlet showing the resolution of London women sending their husbands to fight in the Thirty Years' War, c.1619 (woodcut), English School, (17th century)/Private Collection/The Stapleton Collection/Bridgeman Images; **p39:** Geraint Lewis/ Alamy Stock Photo; **p42:** Alastair Muir/REX/Shutterstock; **p44, 49:** Donald Cooper/Photostage; **p51:** ITV/REX/Shutterstock; **p54, 58:** Donald Cooper/Photostage; **p63:** Leemage/Getty Images; **p66, 69:** Donald Cooper/Photostage; **p74:** Chronicle/ Alamy Stock Photo; **p79:** Carol Rosegg/Shakespeare Theatre Company; **p82:** Geraint Lewis/Alamy Stock Photo; **p87:** Geraint Lewis/REX/Shutterstock; **p92. 99, 102:** Donald Cooper/ Photostage.

Every effort has been made to contact copyright holders of material reproduced in this book. Any omissions will be rectified in subsequent printings if notice is given to the publisher.

Extracts are from William Shakespeare: *Othello*, Oxford School Shakespeare edited by Roma Gill (OUP, 2009)

We are grateful for permission to reprint the following copyright texts:

John Bayley: extract from 'Tragedy and Consciousness: Othello' in *Shakespeare and Tragedy* (RKP, 1981), copyright © John Bayley 1981, reprinted by permission of Taylor & Francis Books UK.

Anthony Brennan: extracts from *Shakespeare's Dramatic Structures* (RKP, 1986), copyright © Anthony Brennan 1986, reprinted by permission of Taylor & Francis Books UK.

Michael Billington: extract from 'Othello review - history is made with the RSC's fresh take on the tragedy', *The Guardian*, theguardian.com, 12 June 2015, copyright © Guardian News & Media Ltd 2015, reprinted by permission of GNM.

Paul Edmondson: extract on Desdemona from bloggingshakespeare.com, reprinted by permission of the author.

T S Eliot: extract from *Shakespeare and the Stoicism of Seneca* (OUP for the Shakespeare Association, 1927), reprinted by permission of Faber & Faber Ltd.

G Wilson Knight: extracts from 'The Othello Music' in *The Wheel of Fire: Essays on interpretation of Shakespeare's tragedy* (2e, Routledge, 2005), copyright © G Wilson Knight 1930, reprinted by permission of Taylor & Francis Books UK.

F R Leavis: extract from 'Diabolic Intellect and the Noble Hero' in *The Common Pursuit* (Faber, 2008), first published in Scrutiny 6, 1937, reprinted by permission of Faber & Faber Ltd.

David Lister: extract from review of Othello, 'Can it be wrong to "black up" for Othello?', *The Independent*, 6 Aug 1997, copyright © The Independent 1997, reprinted by permission of Independent Print Ltd/ ESI Media.

Ian McKellen: extract on Iago from www.mckellen.com, reprinted by permission of Ian McKellen c/o Independent Talent, London.

Stephen Moss: extract from review, 'Adrian Lester and Rory Kinnear: Othello and Iago are a bit cracked', *The Guardian*, theguardian.com, 10 April 2013, copyright © Guardian News &Media Ltd 2013, reprinted by permission of GNM.

Karen Newman: '"And wash the Ethiop white": Femininity and the monstrous in Othello' in *Fashioning Femininity and English Renaissance Drama* (Univ of Chicago Press, 2009), reprinted by permission of the University of Chicago.

Charles Spencer: extracts from review of Othello at the National Theatre, *The Telegraph*, 24 April 2013, copyright © Telegraph Media Group Ltd 2013, reprinted by permission of TMG.

John Wain: extract from his introduction to *Shakespeare: Othello* (Casebook Series) edited by John Wain (Palgrave Macmillan, 1994